Resource Book

Resource Book

DOUG HEWITT
& ROBIN HEWITT

PRUFROCK PRESS INC.
WACO, TEXAS

Library of Congress Cataloging-in-Publication Data

Hewitt, Doug.
 Free college resource book / Doug Hewitt and Robin Hewitt.
   p. cm.
 Includes bibliographical references.
 ISBN-13: 978-1-59363-381-3 (pbk.)
 ISBN-10: 1-59363-381-5 (pbk.)
 1. Student aid--United States. 2. Scholarships--United States. 3. Student financial aid administration. 4.
College choice--United States. I. Hewitt, Robin, 1957- II. Title.
  LB2337.4.H49 2010
  378.30973
                              2009042626

Copyright © 2010, Prufrock Press Inc.
Edited by Lacy Compton
Cover and Layout Design by Marjorie Parker

ISBN-13: 978-1-59363-381-3
ISBN-10: 1-59363-381-5

Printed in the United States of America.

At the time of this book's publication, all facts and figures cited are the most current available. All telephone
numbers, addresses, and Web site URLs are accurate and active. All publications, organizations, Web sites, and
other resources exist as described in the book, and all have been verified. The authors and Prufrock Press Inc.
make no warranty or guarantee concerning the information and materials given out by organizations or content
found at Web sites, and we are not responsible for any changes that occur after this book's publication. If you
find an error, please contact Prufrock Press Inc.

Prufrock Press Inc.
P.O. Box 8813
Waco, TX 76714-8813
Phone: (800) 998-2208
Fax: (800) 240-0333
http://www.prufrock.com

For our five children, who put in the time to
pursue their dreams

Contents

Introduction 1

1 Career Choices 9

2 How What You Do (Inside and Outside the Classroom) Influences Scholarship Money 21

3 Skill Sets and Scholarship Money 31

4 What's Your Major? 45

5 Choosing a College 59

6 Finding Information 77

7 Tools to Dig Up the Money 91

8 How to Get Going 101

9 Write a Winning Essay 111

10 Scholarship Application Sessions 123

11 The Interview 133

12 Tricks of the Trade 141

13 After the Money Rolls In 151

Resources 159

References 187

About the Authors 191

Introduction

"And now the pitcher holds the ball, and now he lets it go,
And now the air is shattered by the force of Casey's blow."
Casey at the Bat
by Ernest Lawrence Thayer

Why Do I Need This Book?

THERE are two simple reasons. The first reason is that college costs are escalating. The second reason is that we can show you how to get free college funding.

Have you ever wondered how many high school graduates go on to enroll in college or at a university? Of the students graduating from high school in 2008, 68.6% enrolled in college (Bureau of Labor Statistics, 2009). With so many students going on to higher education, the sources of funding can get stretched thin.

But the benefits of a college degree are apparent. Especially during tough economic times, the advantage of a college degree can be seen in the unemployment rate. In October 2008, the unemployment rate for high school graduates stood at 26.7%. Young male college graduates had an 8.7% unemployment rate while young female college graduates had a 6.6% unemployment rate

(Bureau of Labor Statistics, 2009). This disparity highlights the rewards of a college education.

Still, the cost of attending college has been rising steadily. Since the 1997–1998 academic year, the annual average cost of tuition, fees, room, and board have increased 30% at public institutions and 23% at private institutions *after* adjusting prices for inflation (Snyder, Dillow, & Hoffman, 2009).

Pursuing a college degree is a sound financial decision, despite escalating college expenses. Of course, there are other benefits to college, such as social, intellectual, and emotional development, but the financial benefits are well documented. The Census Bureau projected the lifetime earnings of a college graduate and a high school graduate. The difference is eye-opening. In a 2002 study titled *The Big Payoff: Educational Attainment and Synthetic Estimates of Work-Life Earnings*, the lifetime earnings in 1999 dollars were projected to be $2.1 million for a person with a 4-year degree but only $1.2 million for a worker with only a high school diploma (Day & Newburger, 2002).

It probably doesn't require a lot of convincing to know that a college education can be expensive. And the benefits to earning potentials can be obvious to anyone taking a detailed look at the want ads (at least the ones that list salaries). Many people, though, don't realize just how much financial aid is available.

The majority of undergraduate students receive financial aid. The U.S. Department of Education published a study titled the *2007–08 National Postsecondary Student Aid Study* (Wei et al., 2009). In it, statistics showed the value of applying for financial aid. Sixty-six percent of undergraduates received some kind of financial aid. For those who received aid, the average amount was $9,100. This included loans and state and institutional aid (Wei et al., 2009). According to the same study, 52% of students who received aid were awarded grants, which averaged $4,900.

As we'll show in this book, college funds are available from different sources. There are federal, state, and institutional sources.

The *2007–08 National Postsecondary Student Aid Study* (Wei et al., 2009) reported that 47% of undergraduates received federal aid, which averaged $6,600. State grants averaged $2,500 and went to 16% of undergraduates. Institutional grants went to 20% of undergraduates and averaged $5,000.

This Book's Audience

This book is written for students who are looking for college funding, although we're sure there'll be some parents who will read it, too. The reason we address students in this book is because we believe in giving them responsibility for this process.

Whether you are a parent or a student, we encourage everybody reading this book to read all sections. As a parent, you want to understand the challenges and perspective of finding funding from the student's position. As a student, you want to understand what your parents can do to help.

What We Mean by "College" and "Scholarship"

We use a little shorthand in this book. It would get tedious if, every time we want to say "an institution of higher education," we had to spell out that we mean any educational situation beyond high school, whether it's a trade school, a community college, a 4-year college, a university, or an online degree program.

Instead, we'll just use the term *college*. So when we say we can help you go to college for free, we mean we can help you find funding for whichever educational setting you're looking at.

But what about the term *scholarship*? We also use the term in a very generic way. We're really talking about a source of money. But whenever we use the term scholarship, we'll be talking about *free* money. We'll talk a bit about loans, but we will never call a loan a scholarship.

Throughout the book, we include "Scholarship Spotlight"

sections that highlight interesting scholarships, such as the listing for the $1,000 scholarship based on an essay on social nudity. Many are fun to read about, even if they don't fall under your individual bailiwick. We also include some spotlights on more established scholarships that have a wider audience. We encourage students to apply for as many scholarships as they can and keep their minds open when searching.

Also in the book, we include "Cash Clue" sections that will be little nuggets of information to help you in your quest to fund college. For example, we suggest having highlighters handy when you read through funding material (including this book!) so you can highlight any section or passage that is of special interest to you.

Scholarship Money Available

According to the Illinois Student Assistance Commission (2009), a resident student's average cost in the 2008–2009 academic year was more than $18,000 annually for a public 4-year college and more than $37,000 for a private college.

Depressing numbers, right? With these high costs of college, many parents find themselves withdrawing from their retirement accounts and taking out second mortgages. But there's good news! There's more than $134 billion available in scholarship money (Pope, 2007). We'll help you get some of that money.

Why We Wrote This Book

A few years ago, when Doug's daughter was a high school senior, she came home one day and mentioned there would be a parent meeting with the counselors to go over the FAFSA. "What's a FAFSA?" Doug asked. His daughter shrugged and added, "Something you need for college." When Doug went to this meeting, he found that only five other parents had shown up—out of a senior class of more than 300 students. When he researched the

FAFSA (Free Application for Federal Student Aid), he learned that many of the books on the subject were too dense to easily digest.

Four years later, we had five children attending higher education, all at no cost to us. Our research, exploration, and parenting savvy have helped us guide our children to find the right careers, schools, and necessary funding. Our experiences will help you in your search for success in higher education.

We could tell you we set out to have five children and then devised a plan to have them all attending institutions of higher education with no cost to us. Yes, we could say that, but it would be a lie.

Like most people, there are some aspects of our lives that we planned; others just happened. We did plan to get married, of course, bringing together our families of two and three children, giving us that magical number of five kids. But with finances and the job market in flux, with gas prices and inflation taking more than our annual raises, financially we ended up taking one year, one month, and one week at a time. So when our first child applied for college admission, we began a crash course in figuring out how to help her find scholarships to pay for it.

We had one thing going for us. Although we hadn't any concrete plans for funding our children in higher education, we knew some basic tenets for how scholarship money was awarded—and we practiced these tenets. Well, that's part of the story.

You see, we stumbled upon a secret of raising children to be well-rounded adults. And guess what? That's what colleges are looking for. Sure, they looked for talented individuals as well, and that's why we made sure we exposed our children to as many different experiences as possible, helping them to find their natural interests and what their natural talents allowed them to excel at. Perhaps not all that surprisingly, this helped our children win scholarships.

We hope to give you some of our secrets and tips and at the same time show how these approaches can help you win that scholarship money.

We understand that it's not easy. But we've been through the process, and we can help. We also know about what works in the larger sense. This book isn't a list of scholarships and instructions telling you to apply for them. Those kinds of books are OK, but they don't help much in telling you how to win those scholarships and what kind of game plan to have. We'll give you a game plan and show you how to keep motivated. Keep an open mind, and we'll help guide you to the promised land of full college funding.

What's Up With the GRAND SLAM?

When we started organizing the material for this book, we ran into a lot of acronyms. Sometimes they're useful, sometimes they're a headache. We realized, though, that we could summarize our game plan for winning college scholarships with the acronym GRAND SLAM. Now, for those who don't play or watch baseball, a grand slam is hitting a home run when the bases are loaded. It's knocking one out of the park. And you can knock one out of the park with our GRAND SLAM approach to winning scholarships.

Get started now.
Research yourself, your interests, and your skills.
Analyze the fit/match between you and the college.
Navigate your way to scholarship money.
Develop an action plan.

Scholarships—find the ones you can win.
Learn how to write good essays.
Apply for scholarships and for admission to the college
    that's right for you.
Maintain your advantage by following up.

We'll talk more about the GRAND SLAM in the course of this book, and we're sure it will help you with college funding.

Tricks of the Trade

Along with our GRAND SLAM method to help you find college funding, we have populated this book with tricks of the trade to help you. Our strategy will help you get your funding, because we take you through the complete process. We've discovered many students don't know where to start.

So we'll take you there, one step at a time, and give you tricks of the trade to better your chances of winning those scholarships. Some of the tricks of the trade we'll tell you about include:

- ✓ scheduling a time and day each week for working on college choices and scholarships;
- ✓ keeping journals;
- ✓ maintaining computer files and organization strategies;
- ✓ updating progress charts;
- ✓ using books correctly by writing in the margins, taking notes, and using self-adhesive notes; and
- ✓ writing to-do lists.

Some Basic Acronyms

With any bureaucracy come acronyms. It's a universal rule, like the Second Law of Thermodynamics. With so much money at stake, it seems like the system would be designed to give students the best opportunity possible to understand the process and not be intimidating. That's not necessarily the case! We'll give you some basic acronyms to get you started, although you'll probably run into more as you conduct your search for scholarship money. We suggest you find out what each acronym means and write the meaning in a notebook for later reference.

AP—Advanced Placement
EFC—Expected Family Contribution
FAFSA — Free Application for Federal Student Aid

FSEOG—Federal Supplemental Educational Opportunity Grant

GPA—Grade Point Average

NMSQT— National Merit Scholarship Qualifying Test

PSAT/NMSQT—Preliminary SAT/National Merit Scholarship Qualifying Test

SAR—Student Aid Report

URL—Uniform Resource Locator

Get Ready

This book can help you succeed in college, but you're going to have to do the work. Reading alone won't produce a single college or scholarship acceptance letter. Unless you actually sit down and write an essay, you won't win any scholarships that require an essay in the application. We'll make it as easy as we can, but ultimately you're the one who's going to achieve results.

We hope you not only enjoy reading this book, we hope it leads you to a successful career, starting with a college degree that was fully funded by sources other than your bank account. We would love to hear from you. Let us know how this book helped you.

1

Career Choices

So, What Do You Want to Be When You Grow Up?

WE hope at some point you've thought about different careers. Although it's fine to go to college with an undeclared major, it's extremely helpful to have a general idea of the track you wish to pursue. How many people do you know with no idea what their dreams careers are? We'll bet it's plenty. So we've included some great strategies for helping you think about careers.

Of course, as parents, we understand there are other considerations. Not only do you want to make decisions that might have the biggest financial payoff down the road, you want emotional payoffs, too. Remember, money isn't everything! Satisfying careers can be low paying. Many people enjoy volunteer work or running a nonprofit organization. You want job satisfaction—to be happy doing what you do. Otherwise, you'll spend years doing a job that provides little personal satisfaction. You want a career you're proud of. That's what we want for our own children, and it's what we'll help you achieve.

Imagine trying out for a baseball team and not knowing what position you want to play and for what position you have the most talent. These aren't always the same, of course. Sometimes you want to play shortstop, but you don't have the natural skills to field ground balls. But if you want to play that position, you can practice.

In the same way, you might have a natural ability for math, but you want to go into the visual arts. Again, practice will help you achieve what you want. By all means, you need to know if you're a "people person" before launching a career in sales.

One thing is certain: You need to assess your skills and, actually, yourself. These kinds of questions will come up in scholarship applications, so by doing your homework now, you'll be prepared to win those scholarships.

Where does a person start when considering higher education? This chapter!

Cash Clue

Not all is lost if you're not naturally gifted. Whether it's sports or math, you can improve with practice!

Three Big Questions

What do you *want* to do?

What do you *like* to do?

What are you *good* at?

These questions are sometimes not easy to answer. There's an entire industry built around the need for self-assessment. We don't have to pay anyone, though, to tell us these things.

You might have an ironclad notion of where your career path will take you. Good for you! The majority of people, however, have ideas that are fuzzy at best.

Cash Clue

Take a step back and think "big picture" for a moment. Maybe you've already focused on a career. Open your mind (*ohhmmm* . . .) and consider different possibilities. Write down 10 other careers and why you would or wouldn't consider them.

Why Having an Idea of Career Choice Helps

Why do you need to know what your future career might be? Here are just a few reasons why:

1. If your career choice is unclear, you might end up in a job you hate.
2. Scholarship applications often ask for information about what you want to do with your life, especially with regard to a career. A firm career in mind will assist in the scholarship application process.
3. Colleges and universities often have certain curriculums that are nationally recognized as being superior. Knowing what career to pursue can affect your choice of college and help you to avoid making a poor decision.
4. Having a career goal might motivate you to get better grades, and good grades mean a higher GPA.
5. You'll be able to finally answer the question, "What do you want to be when you grow up?"

When to Start

It's really never too early to consider the big issues of career choice and skill assessment. If you know what you want to do, you're much more likely to get good grades to achieve your goal—and getting a career is definitely a goal. Not everybody who wants to be a doctor gets to be one. Medical schools turn down applicants in droves, and the training is arduous.

The eighth grade is a good grade to start considering your career and skills. If you're thinking about working as a NASCAR mechanic, college prep classes might not be the best choice. You can start planning to take the appropriate courses when you start high school.

Another point to consider: Many people assume that scholarships are distributed only to high school seniors. Wrong! If you're starting early, whether in grade school or at some point before your senior year, there are scholarships you can apply for.

By the time you're a senior in high school, you're already on the brink of the college admission and scholarship season. The paperwork alone can be daunting (and discouraging!).

If you're not yet in high school, start now!

If you're in high school, but not a senior, start now!

If you're a high school senior, start as early as you can. (Like, "*right now!*")

Scholarship Spotlight

The Alliance for Young Artists & Writers offers numerous scholarships to young artists and writers, including $10,000 scholarships to high school seniors who earn National Portfolio Gold Medals. Other scholarships can vary from $500 to full tuition (Alliance for Young Artists & Writers, 2009). For more details, visit http://www.artandwriting.org.

Career Choice, Pros and Cons

This book can't do your work for you. You're going to have to sit down and ask yourself the questions we pose in the book.

We've discovered that setting up a pro/con list can help us to at least narrow down the answers to any tough question we're facing.

Get a piece of paper and write down 10 career possibilities in a column. Add two other columns, one for pros and one for cons. Fill in any pros and cons you can think of.

Show the list to your friends. See if they can think of any pros and cons that you haven't considered. Counselors and teachers can be approached, too. We've found that they're in that profession for a reason—they enjoy helping students, so take advantage of that! Parents, too, can be a resource. They often have a better understanding of the financial pros and cons of certain careers than you might expect.

For example, you might list dentist as a career. In the pro column you could list good pay, good job security, good schedule, and helps people. In the con column, you could list extra college years needed, cost of insurance, can be repetitive, and need to be available for emergencies. For a journalist, the pros could be covering interesting events and seeing your name in print, while the cons could be a low starting pay and difficulty in breaking into the field. For a computer programmer, the pros could be good job outlook and good schooling available with the cons being the potential to get lonely in front of a computer all day and the need to keep updated with training on new applications. You get the idea. A sample list is provided in Figure 1.

Cash Clue
We'll discuss tools of the trade later, but we'll spill the beans a little here and let you know one tool is a folder. Put your pro/con list in it for later reference and updating.

Of course, some aspects of a particular job will appear on some people's pro list and on others' con list. This list is meant to help you, and there are no hard and fast rules. Whatever works for you, do it.

	Pros	Cons
Dentist	good pay good job security good schedule	extra college insurance cost repetitive
Computer Programmer	job outlook school available advancement	must stay current stare at monitor all day

Figure 1. Sample career choice pro and con list.

Here are some other considerations for your pro/con list:

✓ Is it an indoor job? Outdoor? Will you work in a cubicle, in an office, or in a high-tech lab?

✓ How well does the job pay starting out? How about after a few years on the job? What about after 20 years of experience?

✓ Does the job entail working with others or are you sitting in front of a computer all day? Which would you prefer?

✓ Is there any travel associated with the job?

✓ How much independence will you have?

✓ Is this a kind of job being outsourced overseas?

✓ Can you get this job anywhere in the country or will you have to move to a specific area?

✓ How much education is needed? Will you need to continue with schooling throughout your career to keep up with industry trends?

Self-Assessment

You probably know some of the things you're good at and some not so much. Maybe you're a great dancer. Does that help with your career-making decision? That depends. Maybe you love

Strengths	Weaknesses	Skills
writing	social skills	mechanically inclined
hard worker	hand-eye coordination	athletic
attention to detail	financial planning	writing computer applications
math		

Figure 2. Strengths, weaknesses, and skills self-assessment.

dancing and you want to run a small business such as a dance school. In that case, it definitely helps to dance well! (Imagine taking a dance lesson and seeing your instructor stumbling around, stepping on toes.)

The point here is that you shouldn't worry about listing items that appear unrelated at first glance. Write down everything you're good at. Are you a skilled conversationalist? Maybe you could consider a job with conflict negotiations, sales, or an employee relations department.

OK, time to take out your notebook again. This time, label three columns as strengths, weaknesses, and skills (see Figure 2). Be honest! This is to help you, and you don't have to show it to a soul. For example, under strengths you might list writing and hard worker. Under weaknesses you could list not good with people and math. Under skills you might list mechanically inclined and athletic.

Hang on to this list—you'll use it in a minute.

Cash Clue

Searching online for "best paying job" and "computer career" and other word combinations is a great way to come across careers you might not have otherwise thought of.

Combining the Lists

Now it's time to look at your list of career choices and see if your strengths, weaknesses, and skills match up. If you want feedback, this is a great time to talk to a high school counselor. You also can contact the college you're considering, locate a department faculty member, and fire off an e-mail asking if your strengths and weaknesses are in line with someone in that field of study.

If you feel good that your ideal career jibes well with your strengths, weaknesses, and skills—great! Read on. If not, get feedback, rinse, and repeat.

A Question to Ask

OK, so you have an idea of what you want to do, at least in general, and you have some idea of your skill sets. Now is the time to find someone who is actually working in that career field and ask, "What are the three things I should know about going into this field that I probably don't know now?"

Cash Clue

If your parent has any friends (or friends of friends) working in a career field you're considering, ask if that friend will talk about it to you.

The Career Folder and Notebook

As you move ahead in your planning, you'll want to keep records. You'll want to know what led you to make certain decisions.

It's important that you have a notebook and a file folder. You can cut out (from magazines and newspapers) or print (from the Internet) articles describing careers to go into your folder. In your notebook, you can write down your pro/con lists, and we suggest adding a journal-style (dated) entry every now and then and explain to yourself why you haven't changed your mind about your career path, or explain to yourself why you might be starting to lean in another direction.

Exploring Options

Unless you've always known what you want to do, keep your options open for as long as possible. There's no need to commit to a particular course right away. What if you change your mind? Use your journal/notebook and continue to make entries. Whenever you meet someone who works in a field you considered at one time (but perhaps veered away from), talk about your choices. At the very least, you'll get a good feeling that you've made the right choice.

OK, How About a Day Job?

Let's say you want to write bestselling novels. If you're successful, you probably will earn enough money from that to live on. The same goes for being a world-renown musician. However, the odds are against you. Most beginning artists have "day jobs," which pay enough to support their true love of playing music or writing novels (or painting or whatever).

The same rules apply to your "day job." You might know what career you want, but you have to be realistic. Go for your dreams, but make sure you have a backup plan, your day job, and make sure it's one you like! (Doug's day job lasted 25 years.)

A good example of planning for a day job is our youngest son. He loves to play trombone and wants to be a professional jazz musician. He's decided to pursue a major in music and take the classes he needs to qualify as a high school music teacher and band director. This way, he'll have nights, weekends, and summers to pursue his dream job.

Why Career Assessments Are Important

The choice of a career or at least a career direction certainly plays an influence of what type of scholarship (and other) money you'll be most likely to win.

It's a lot easier to search for money when you can narrow the field to a specific career or major. Searching online for "physics" will be more productive than looking for "science" and looking for "college money for science" will be more specific than searching for "college money."

Careers that are in the highest demand usually have the highest number of scholarships and grants. Take nursing, for example. In many states there are programs that will pay full tuition for a nursing degree in return for a specific number of years spent nursing in that state after graduation.

How This Affected Us—Two Case Studies

Our daughter Lynn was able to decide on a vocation early in high school: teaching. She had the right skills, and the job suited her demeanor. This allowed Lynn to join the Future Teachers of America and focus on taking high school classes in areas that would specifically benefit her later in college and on scholarship applications. She also took several Advanced Placement classes so that upon entering college she had credits equivalent to a full semester. This was a great achievement to add to her scholarship applications, as it showed she was capable of setting goals and achieving them.

Our son Thomas wanted to serve his country before settling on a career and college. He spent 4 years in the U.S. Marine Corps, learning about himself and gaining experience in different career fields. The experience gleaned in the Marine Corps enabled him to zero in on criminal justice as a major, and he was able to take some college courses while he was on active duty. These course credits were transferable, and he shortened the amount of time he would need to earn his degree after his service period was over. And of course, by joining a branch of the military, he was able to be assured of government financial aid through the GI Bill.

The earlier you can decide on a career, the more opportunity you have of taking advantage of what your high school offers. If you want to be a electrician or mechanic, many high schools offer technical courses off campus where you can take electrical and automotive classes. The same holds for business majors with classes from DECA, the Distributive Education Clubs of America. Showing that you know your future goals will influence scholarship boards in making the decision on whether or not to award you funding.

Career and Financial Trade-offs

It's helpful to consider the general popularity of a career field. Careers that are easier to attain and are pursued by a greater number of people generally will have less free funding available because federal and state programs zero in on the high-need careers. If you want to be, say, an auto mechanic, you might have to look harder for scholarships than if you plan to be a veterinarian. Like with other economic issues, it's a question of supply and demand. The trick is to learn to combine your search for scholarships with careers that match your talents, abilities, hobbies, and interests.

Colleges and Careers

When you're considering specific careers, it's a good idea to check college websites to see what kind of information they have about helping students achieve those careers.

Many colleges now have virtual tours and also will send out information packets. These might give you some ideas about how well suited you are to the career field you have chosen.

The G in GRAND SLAM

Remember our GRAND SLAM acronym? Perhaps the most important letter is the first, G. *G*et started now. If you're starting early, great. It's still important to get started now. Time slips by incredibly fast, and there will be unforeseen roadblocks along the way. If you're getting a late start, you don't have a moment to lose. There are deadlines for scholarship applications, and you need time to gather your resources, time to practice essay writing, and time to choose a college!

So please, get started now. Well, at least as soon as you finish reading this book.

Scholarship Spotlight

The Duck Brand Duct Tape Stuck at Prom Contest offers a $3,000 scholarship to the winning couple that makes their prom outfits out of duct tape ("Duck Brand Duct Tape Stuck at Prom Scholarship Winners," 2009)! For details, visit http://www.stuckatprom.com/contests/prom.

How What You Do (Inside and Outside the Classroom) Influences Scholarship Money

2

Wow, Now That's a Chapter Title!

BUT it expresses what we want to talk about in this chapter. If you think about it, a scholarship application is a series of questions asking for information about you. Yes, there are plenty of scholarships that will require a one-on-one interview, but the interviews usually occur at some point past the first round. That is, out of all of the applications for a particular scholarship, maybe 10 or 20% get approved for the first round. At that point, the remaining candidates might get called in for an interview. Of course, there could be another round or two before an interview occurs, which is how it happened with our daughter Lynn. For her, the third round was the interview round.

The initial application asks questions so that the people with the scholarship money to dole out can find out about you. Scholarship money goes to people in different categories, of course. Some go to people who show the most talent in, say, mathematics. Others might go into a particular profession, such as teaching. Still others are based simply on the best essay on a particular subject.

But for the most part, scholarship applications want to find out who you are and what you've done with your life, both inside and outside the classroom.

Why? Because that's how scholarship judges know (with as much certainty as possible) that the scholarship money is going to the kinds of people for whom the money is intended. For example, they certainly don't want to award scholarships to students who seem destined to drop out of college. Therefore, anything in your background that demonstrates the ability to stick to long-term commitments is a good thing.

Another good point to make regards summer vacations. The activities you participate in during summer vacations can indicate to colleges what you're passionate about (Berger, 2008). Information about summer camps and programs in every area of interest can be found online by doing a search for "summer opportunities."

Scholarship Spotlight

The Harry S. Truman Scholarship Foundation awards scholarship funds up to $30,000 for college juniors who want to pursue graduate degrees in public service fields. The foundation also assists with career counseling and internship placement (Truman Scholarship Foundation, 2009). For more details, visit http://www.truman.gov. Don't forget that you'll want to keep applying for scholarships even after you've entered college!

Things You Did Before Entering High School

Maybe the things you did before entering high school aren't as important as what you've done in your junior and senior years in high school, but they can make a difference in the scholarship selection process. Anything can make a difference in the scholarship application process, so what you can put in your application to give you an edge is desirable for people wanting full college funding for free.

The other thing about what you did before entering high school, and keep this in mind when you start writing essays, is that what you did laid down a foundation for things that came later. For example, if you were in the Cub Scouts and later became a Boy Scout, or the Brownies and the Girl Scouts, this would show commitment and a progression that would look good to scholarship judges.

For preteens, it's a good idea to get involved with community organizations, volunteer work, and sports. Although we're here to help you win scholarship money, we also have a strong desire to help parents raise children who are healthy, well-adjusted, and productive. We involved our children in intramural sports starting in the third grade because we believe sports help children grow into mature, responsible adults by teaching them about teamwork, communication, and how to handle disappointment. One of the most important lessons we hammered home with our kids is that losing a game doesn't make a kid a loser. Everyone loses at one point or another.

When you start the scholarship application process, we'll show you how to approach it. One of the tricks of the trade we'll tell you about is keeping notebooks or word processing files with your relevant information on it. One of the things you'll want to document is your involvement with activities before high school.

Extracurricular Activities

Next to scholastic achievement, participation in extracurricular activities is the most important aspect of scholarship applications. Although we encourage students to get good grades, that should not be an excuse to stay out of participating in other activities. Scholarship judges generally look for well-rounded candidates. Participation in extracurricular activities shows them that you're not one-dimensional. Don't go overboard, though. Dedication to a few organizations and taking leadership roles can count more than simply being on multiple membership lists.

Keep an open mind when you think about the extracurricular activities you participate in. For example, if you've helped out with your church doing volunteer work, list it. For example, our daughter Lynn took on the responsibility of helping out with the daycare at the church. This enabled her to realize that she enjoyed working with children, a fact that would lead her to a career decision to become a teacher. Of course, because she was able to get focused so early, she was able to put together a wonderful scholarship application and won enough to pay her way for 4 years at college.

Cash Clue
It's not too late to do volunteer work that will make your scholarship applications stand out above other applications.

Talent and Drive in Our Children

We're taking a personal approach in this book, hoping that by sharing our experiences, we'll give you ideas with which to win scholarships. And so we want to share our observations about our children and the differences we noted between talent and drive.

Thomas
One of the most remarkable talents that Thomas has is his ability to organize complex tasks. You could unload 20 eighteen-wheelers full of unmarked boxes with a wide array of stock, and within a few days, he could have a logistics program up and

running that would be able to ship an item overnight to anywhere in the world. That's his talent, but his drive was to join the Marine Corps. It was that way ever since he got his first G.I. Joe when he was 9 years old. He ended up in the Marine Corps, of course, and was employed in logistics. With funding provided by the GI Bill, he now attends a community college and plans to go into law enforcement. As anyone who has watched *CSI* or *Forensic Files* knows, analyzing a crime scene requires the analytical and organizational skills that will help Thomas to excel in this field. Eventually, he would like to open his own security business.

Grace

Grace also has a talent that is related to her drive: photography. Perhaps it was our visits to museums when she was younger that instilled a sense of visual art in her. Photography is much more complex than point and click, and Grace understood this at an early age. Her talent and the ability to put together a brilliant portfolio enabled her to get an internship with a major photography studio.

Lynn

We've already talked about Lynn, and how her talent with working with children matched her drive to become a teacher. Her membership in the Future Teachers of America organization helped her to win a teaching fellowship that has paid for her 4 years of college tuition. We should note that some of the scholarship money we talk about in this book comes with a few stipulations. As with most teaching fellowships, after she graduates, Lynn will be required to teach in her state for 4 years to meet her scholarship obligations. But because this was her career goal all along, we look at this as simply a geographical restriction.

Are you noticing a trend?

When talents align well with the drive toward a particular career, good things (such as free college funding) happens.

Scott

Scott has a talent for mathematics and academics in general. He earned all A's on his report cards, and in the 10th grade, he decided to apply to the North Carolina School of Science and Math (NCSSM), a premiere boarding school that only enrolls gifted students. He was accepted at NCSSM and went there for the 11th and 12th grades. Scott automatically received a 4-year scholarship to any North Carolina university upon graduation. He is attending North Carolina State University where he is majoring in physics. He also received scholarships from Boy Scouts and church, as well as a $2,700 scholarship for children of former members of the U.S. Marine Corps (USMC). He has decided to go on to graduate school and is already applying for scholarships to MIT.

Alan

Alan's love of music led him to long hours of practice with his trombone. He attended numerous band camps, receiving instruction from a variety of well-known musicians. He also tried out for all-county bands, where he was usually seated very high. As a high school senior, he auditioned for a spot with the Greensboro Symphony Youth Orchestra in North Carolina and was selected. His love of music and his accompanying talent helped him to win scholarships designed for music majors.

Self-Assessments

Self-assessments are important because they will help you to decide what major to choose in college and what career to pursue, and both of these have an effect on which college you wish to attend. For example, if you're analytical in nature, an engineering college might be the best choice for you.

Self-assessments also will come into play when you start applying for scholarships. Scholarship applications will ask what you

Things I'm Good At	Things I'm Interested In
public speaking	coaching tennis
tennis	creating video games
video games	writing speeches
math quizzes	woodworking

Figure 3. Self-assessment for career interest.

want to accomplish in school (and in life), and self-assessments will help you write answers that are well thought out.

Here is our simple plan for conducting an effective self-assessment: On a blank sheet of paper, make two columns. Make a title for column one: Things I'm Good At. Write down everything that you feel you're good at. If you're a good speaker, write it down. Good at a particular sport? Write it down. For the second column, write down: Things I'm Interested In. Fill in this column with subjects you feel would inspire you to work hard and might be related to what you feel would make a great career for you. See Figure 3 for an example.

Save this for later when you're applying for scholarships and college admissions. It will save you a lot of time, like it did for us.

The Importance of Self-Assessments for Scholarships

We found that the self-assessments were essential background homework for many of the essay questions our children answered. There are some essay questions that simply require some thought such as "What would be your first act as President?" Other questions, though, strike at the heart of the self-assessment. For example, consider the following question: "If you could have any career in the world and money wasn't an issue, what would you do?" Now, isn't it great that you already have completed a list of things that interest you?

Beyond having the list handy, we believe these self-assessments are a work-in-progress. As people get exposed to new situations and experiences, their likes and dislikes evolve. Your list might change, but you'll always be aware of those changes. That change in itself might make for a great essay topic. We want to keep stressing that essays are an extremely important part of the scholarship application. Anything that can give you an edge, such as your thoughtful self-assessments, will help you win scholarship money.

Cash Clue

Some of the skills we talk about are important to not only finding scholarships, they're also important for a student to be successful at college.

Scholarships Sources

We'll get into more detail later about where to go online to hunt for scholarships. For now, keep an open mind about scholarship sources. Always have your eyes and ears open. We didn't find out until Scott's second year in college that there were scholarships available for the children of former U.S. Marine Corps personnel.

As we'll show you, the main sources of scholarship money will be scholarship databases. In some of these, you enter data about yourself, such as your interests and possible college major (the advantage of self-assessments!) and the database presents you with a list of possible matches. Other databases will present you with scholarships listed in categories.

We don't believe definitions are very helpful to finding funding, but we'll go through a few here just to keep everyone on the same page.

✓ A scholarship is a monetary award meant to help further someone's education.

✓ A grant is a monetary award of aid to people who fit certain criteria. For example, there are many minority-based grants.

✓ Some scholarships are institutional. That is, these scholarships go only to students who are attending that particular institution.

✓ There are a lot of scholarships and grants that are need-based. These scholarships are designed to help students who are not financially well off and who might not be able to afford to attend college without the help of scholarship money.

Other scholarships fit into a general category. These could be scholarships based on athletics or intention to enter a particular field of study.

Scholarships are awarded to students involved with Boy Scouts or Girl Scouts, who fit within a particular minority group, who excel at music or sports or academics, who have a proven financial need, who write outstanding essays, and whose parents were employed in the federal government. With so many scholarship opportunities out there, we're surprised that more students don't go at the hunt for scholarships with more zeal.

As you can see, the self-assessments are already starting to make sense when taking a look at the categories of scholarships and grants.

Scholarship Spotlight

The American Sheep Industry Association offers $1,000 and $2,000 awards to promote the versatility of wool fabrics and yarns. Contestants are encouraged to express their creativity in spinning, knitting, sewing, crocheting, and weaving (American Sheep Association, 2009). For more details, visit http://www.sheepusa.org/MIWW_Contest_Information.

3

Skill Sets and Scholarship Money

The R in GRAND SLAM

RESEARCH yourself, your interests, and your skills.

We've talked about this a little already, but it's so important that we're devoting an entire chapter to the subject.

It sounds easy enough. Ask yourself what you like and dislike. Grade yourself on how well you do certain things. But when you're on the fast track to trying to find college funding, with applications waiting to be filled out, and with your entire future rushing at you with gale-force winds, the time needed to do some self-reflection might seem like time ill spent.

But we're here to say that the more you know yourself, the more you can match yourself up with specific scholarships. Our daughter Lynn would not have won a teaching fellowship if she had not been so convincing during the scholarship interview process that she really wanted to teach. And the reason she was so convincing? She'd spent time thinking about what she wanted to do with her life, what she liked, and what kind of skill sets she had.

So, although we encourage people to apply for many scholarships, we also think it's worthwhile to take the time to research yourself.

Scholarship Spotlight

The Coca-Cola Scholars Foundation awards $3.4 million annually to scholarship recipients through two separate programs. More than 250 scholarships are given to students in high school and community colleges each year (The Coca-Cola Scholars Foundation, 2009). For more details, visit http://www.coca-colascholars.org.

Who Are You?

It's a question that goes unasked. Oh, they'll ask for your name and what your grades are and where you've worked and what clubs you belong to. They ask for personal and professional data. Phone number, social security number, the number of siblings—you name it. Applications are full of questions, and you'll be spending many a night filling them out.

Cash Clue

Copy and paste questions and answers into a text file. If you want to be really efficient, organize the questions into categories such as employment, scholarship, extracurricular activities, and essay-style questions. Then, copy and paste into other applications to your heart's content in order to save gobs of time.

These questions are all designed to find out more about you, of course. There are even some essay questions that are more to the point in asking you to describe yourself. But we've never seen the question phrased so simply: Who are you?

Perhaps Popeye said it best: "I y'am what I y'am."

But we're asking you to expand on that. More than just a little. What are your dreams? What do you think you could stand doing each workday for the rest of your life? What kind of work would inspire you? If you're totally a couch potato, maybe you should rephrase the question into: What job would motivate you most to turn off the TV and get off the couch?

An Important Point to Make

OK, we hope that you ask yourself about your dreams, but we want you to be realistic, too. For example, if you want to write the next Great American Novel, we wish you all the best. Ever hear of the term "starving artist?" That category has quite a plethora of people who want to write novels that are bestsellers.

We're writers ourselves, so we have a little experience in this area, and we can safely say that the vast majority of writers don't make a living at it. In fact, the majority don't sell anything, not an article, not a story, let alone a novel. But that doesn't mean we deny our dreams. We just put them on the side burner while we get a career, jobs that could be considered safer when it comes to the subject of a steady income. We call those our "day jobs."

But if you enjoy playing the part of starving artist, that's fine. Just be honest with yourself. Selling art (and the novel is an art form, believe us) is as difficult as performing a successful brain surgery. There are years and years of training involved, an internship, and who knows what else before the American Medical Association would qualify you to perform a brain surgery. Writing a novel is equally hard, but there's no association that bestows the status of "qualified" on you.

A Case in Point

Scott loves to play his electric guitar. He's quite good, and he might one day make a living at playing it. But being the intelligent kid that he is, he knows that many musicians have day jobs. And being realistic, he understands that to get a good day job—one that he enjoys, one in an industry that is likely to be around in 20 years, and one that offers decent compensation—well, for that he understands that he needs a college degree.

When Scott discovered he was talented in science and math early in his high school career and realized he enjoyed it (although perhaps not as much as playing guitar, which he wasn't introduced to until later), it gave him a head start on deciding what direction his career decision would take.

One day, a representative of the North Carolina School of Science and Mathematics visited his high school. The school sends a representative out to state high schools in order to let students know about its programs. Scott's ears perked up when he was told that students who graduate from the school get free tuition at any public university in the state of North Carolina. Because he was a straight-A student and found high school boring, he decided to apply.

Cash Clue

Be vigilant about researching and staying up to date on any college funding you're able to win. Although many scholarships are renewable, some can be affected by new legislation. For example, lawmakers in the state of North Carolina recently cut state scholarships that had already been awarded. We encourage everyone to be aware that scholarship sources can dry up.

The North Carolina School of Science and Mathematics boards its students on campus. One of the required courses teaches students study skills, that is, how to learn independently on a college level. Scott was able to choose from multiple science classes, enabling him to realize how much he enjoyed physics and ultimately guiding him toward a career in that field.

By zeroing in on a career field in 11th grade, he was able to weigh various colleges in depth and get input from his physics professor.

Having decided early on his major, he was able to increase his chances of receiving extra funding because his scholarship applications were focused on what he wanted to accomplish in college.

It's a wise student who doesn't answer "get a degree" to the question of what a he or she wants to accomplish in college. That answer does nothing to distinguish you from anyone else with aspirations of higher education and will not get you singled out for scholarship money.

How to Research Yourself

There could very well be other ways to do this, but we're telling you how we did it. And, being writers, our methods involve writing, of course. If you haven't gotten yourself a couple of notebooks yet, get them. You'll be using one to track scholarships, and for this purpose, one to research yourself. Of course, a text file on your computer works just as well.

Continue with your list that has the column title Things I'm Good At.

Write down everything. If you're good at telling a joke, write that. If you have a knack for decorating a wall, write it down. The key here is to write everything. This will help you understand where your interests are and what talents you have.

It's good to keep in mind that you might write down some things that you're good at but not great at. That's OK. That's one reason to go to college: to improve the skills that you have. And by researching yourself, you'll have the confidence to answer scholarship application questions with a degree of certainty that many applications lack.

Another good strategy is to talk to parents, teachers, and guidance counselors. Ask them to give you an honest assessment of where they think your talents lie. This will give you food for thought, and you can write down your reflections on the assessments in your journal.

In another section of your journal (or a new text file), list all of the clubs you've been a member of, all of the churches you've attended, and all of the organizations you've joined. Search your memory and ask your parents for help because it's easy to forget about that one summer club you joined for a few months. But that club will have given you some life experience, and that's what you're trying to chronicle so you can evaluate yourself.

Another Case in Point

When our daughter Grace was in high school, she couldn't decide what she wanted to do and did not go straight to college. It wasn't until years later that her interests sharpened into focus.

Because she was unable to identify her aptitudes and skills, she simply decided to go for a job that earned her the highest possible income. That's a decision many people make, and it works out for some. But for Grace, like many others, she ended up unhappy in her profession. Perhaps miserable is a better word.

Sure, some will argue that there are a lot of workers who don't love what they do but still have to make a living. True enough, but we would point out that life is a journey, not a destination, and throughout the course of life, it's good to revisit those journals and think about possible changes in order to get a sense of job satisfaction.

Grace backtracked to what she really enjoyed doing: photography. She explored the different types of photography. She didn't want to focus on photographing nature or children. She considered going into the journalism side of photography, but she wasn't much of a news junkie (like we are). She did have a flare for the dramatic, though, and enjoyed capturing moments that could later be relived, so she ultimately decided on wedding photography.

The availability of career-related scholarship money is directly related, in part, to what kind of demand there is for professionals in that career. Photography is a profession for which there is not a high demand, and Grace found a general absence of scholarship money available for her photography schooling.

While browsing through scholarship opportunities, Grace found that the state she lived in has a scholarship program for Native American tribal members who are at least one quarter Native descent. Although Grace didn't qualify, it reminded her that she is a registered member of a Federally Recognized Native American Tribe, which spurred her into looking for other tribal opportunities. She found that she qualified for several tribal grants and scholarships and that she could declare herself a minority on other scholarship applications.

We helped her to research the field of photography and found that many professional photography studios employ students as assistants for their full-time employees. The pay is average, but it's income! And for a student, any income is good income.

The combination of internship and scholarships enabled Grace to get on-the-job training to augment her college classes. She earned extra spending money, fully financed her education, and learned her trade from experts.

Hone Your Skills

When you come up with your list of skills, it's important to remember that you'll be applying for scholarships based on those skills. Let's look at a few examples of how you can hone your skills and how this will affect your scholarship applications.

If your skill is writing, and you intend to major in English, it pays to write every day—writing in your journal, practicing essays, and even sending letters to friends and family. As with any other skill, practice will result in improvement. If you're hoping for an athletic scholarship, practice the sport. If you're going into business, attend chamber of commerce meetings and find a local Jaycees chapter. Once you join the chapter, get involved with any business projects it's sponsoring.

If you're not counting on any of your skills to win scholarships, we suggest you work at making writing one of your skills. It will pay off for you, not only with improved scholarship opportunities, but you'll find that you'll be able to get better grades in college because writing is such a vital aspect of many college courses. Most colleges require new students to take a freshman English course. You'll have a leg up on that course by working on your writing skills!

How Alan Honed His Skills

When you come up with your list of skills, it's important to remember that you'll be applying for scholarships based on those skills.

Alan, who is majoring in music and education, focused his life on playing his trombone. Early in his high school career, he joined the school's concert band and the marching band. Alan was lucky because his high school band director believed in participating in as many band competitions as possible. These competitions helped hone his skills because playing for trophies makes for more intense practice sessions than playing for visiting grandparents.

He also auditioned for all-county bands. His experience with the Greensboro Symphony Youth Orchestra gave him the benefit of exposure to world-class instructors. It also gave him the opportunity to play with other teenagers who were very talented.

Let's look at that last point a little closer. Alan learned a lot with the Greensboro Symphony Youth Orchestra, much more than we as his tin-ear parents could teach him. But one of the things Alan told us was that he was astonished by the talent level of some of the teenagers in this orchestra. We live in a small town, and although there are many talented individuals that attend his high school, it's just not the same as when an orchestra draws its individuals from a talent pool several states wide.

It can be discouraging when your eyes are opened to how much competition is out there in the real world, but as we pointed out, playing in the same orchestra as those talented individuals would help improve his skills and pay off for him.

When applying for music scholarships, students are sometimes required to play a live performance. Most require a recording of a student's performance. By playing in the orchestra and doing everything he could to hone his skills, Alan's recordings and performances for admission into college and accompanying scholarships were top-notch. He was accepted into a university with a well-known music department, a department that severely limits the number of students going into the program, and won scholarship money as a result.

The Nature of Some Other Scholarships

Some of the scholarships we've discussed so far in this chapter are related to a skill set. We've talked about how to improve those skills to improve your position in winning those scholarships. Many scholarships, though, aren't necessarily based on specific skills.

It any case, it's good idea to take a long look at who is sponsoring the scholarship and do some investigative work. For example, if the scholarship is sponsored by a specific business or organization, it helps to do a bit of research on the organization. What is its business mission statement? How was the scholarship started? Why? For example, if the grant was founded to help give back to the community, it might be a good idea to show in your application (the essay is a good place to do this) that you volunteer and give back to your own community. If the scholarship was designed to help students expand their horizons, you might slant your application to note how the scholarship would not only help you, but it also would enable you to help others to expand their horizons.

Knowing the scholarship's sponsor also should guide you in answering any essay question in the application. We'll devote an entire chapter to writing essays, so don't worry, we'll explain more about our tactics on that front later.

Keep in mind, too, that understanding the aim of the scholarship and the organization that is offering the scholarship can help you save time by not applying for particular scholarships. Sometimes it seems like there's an infinite number of scholarships out there, but you only have a finite amount of time. Don't waste time by applying for scholarships that aren't a good fit. For example, if a scholarship is designed to promote the study of art and the advancement of the artistic community, don't bother if you have no interest in art and you're focusing on a career in business administration.

Sports Scholarships

We had an opportunity to pursue a sports scholarship for both Lynn and Scott. They were great high school athletes. Although they didn't have the skill level or athletic prowess to catch the attention of a large university sports program, they would definitely be competitive at some of the smaller colleges.

We've known people who attended college on sports scholarships, and from our experience, there's a definite trade-off with winning one of them. When on a sports scholarship, you're required to live by the rules of the athletic department and the coach. If you think that means you'll just be practicing and playing just during the season, you're wrong. Even at the smaller colleges, you would be required all year long to attend team meetings, to be a part of the exercise program, and basically do whatever is asked of you.

Some people have no problem with this. If football is your passion and joy and you have the opportunity to attend college for free based on a football scholarship, then by all means give it a go. But our niece, who played collegiate level softball on a scholarship, confided in us that it was difficult to find time to go out on a date because of the time constrictions placed on her. And having enough time to go home on the weekends was difficult at best.

Again, maybe you wouldn't have any objections to these restrictions, but we did want to make sure you understand they exist. If you're considering a sports scholarship, talk to older members on the team and ask about the program's restrictions and requirements.

Scott and Lynn decided that they had other interests that took precedence over a college career that was so focused on athletics. For Lynn, it would have been difficult having the time she needed for all of her teaching functions at college, such as student teaching and her teaching fellowship activities. For Scott, he decided that academics would be a high priority at college, and that he would devote any extra time he had on improving his guitar skills.

But if you really are interested in pursuing a sports scholarship, the two places to start are your high school's coach and athletic director. Let them know about your interests. Many of them have contacts with the coaches of nearby colleges. They could invite one of them to come to a game and take a look at your performance.

Don't be disappointed if your coach and athletic director aren't enthusiastic. They understand there is a lot of competition for these scholarships, and they might not want to go out on a limb for a scholarship that isn't a sure thing.

Instead, you may want to create a video that shows your highlights to the college coaches. If you're not a videographer, talk to classmates or parents and find someone who can help you. You'll want to record as many games and competitions as possible so you can have many highlights in your video. After your performances have been recorded, use editing software to create a file with your highlights. You'll want to give a short speech, about 30 seconds or so, at the start and at the end of the video in order to explain why you made the recording. Explain how passionate you are about the sport, how you're willing to devote the hours of practice time needed to excel, and how you would like the opportunity to perform at the collegiate level. After the highlights, thank the viewer for watching and say the name of your high school.

Hand-deliver your videos to the athletic departments at the

colleges you're interested in. If possible, meet the coach in person and explain why you're there. Be upbeat and optimistic and express a desire to be a part of the coach's program.

This method might not win you a scholarship, but it will increase your chances. And keep in mind, if you don't win an athletic scholarship in your freshman year, you can try out for a practice squad, if there's one available. Ask the coach how you can prove your skills will increase by your sophomore year, and tell him you'll be angling to try out for the team.

Speaking of Videos

Although many scholarship applications can be completed online, there are a few that require their paper applications to be completed with a pen and sent back in. One that our nephew applied for had to be returned in person. It was for a VFW scholarship, and the completed form needed to be returned to a local VFW post.

When you have an opportunity like this, it doesn't hurt to make a video presentation of yourself. Explain your educational goals, your career dreams, and how the scholarship money would help you to reach them. The same holds true for applying for college admission, but we'll talk about that later. For a scholarship video presentation of yourself, keep it short. We suggest no longer than a minute, and make sure you write down the length of the video on the disk. Keeping it short will increase the chances that it will be looked at seriously. Also, put your name on the disk along with an appropriate title such as "Jill Q. Public—Academic and Career Goals."

A one-minute video is plenty of time to briefly talk about your accomplishments. Remember, you want to hit on the highlights, not summarize everything you ever did. List the clubs you're a member of. If you're a member of a church, mention it. If you ever were a volunteer or were involved in a community project, talk about how you are proud to have participated. Mention any academic honors you've received. You get the idea. But you want to lead up to the end of your video presentation, when you'll suggest that your high school career was setting the stage for what you want to accomplish in college.

Cash Clue

Pick an appropriate background such as a bookcase for your video presentation speech. If you have any awards, put them out. Frame any newspaper accounts of your accomplishments. You can show them to the camera during your presentation.

A Word About Loans

Although we're focused on helping you find free college money, we feel like we should talk a little about loans. Often, the college you plan to attend will offer you access to loans if you don't earn enough in scholarships to cover college costs. If you don't meet your scholarship and grant goals by the time you're ready for orientation, don't panic. Part of the financial aid package that you received for the college when you were accepted contains information about loans.

The most common is the Stafford Loan, which is a government loan program for students. You can borrow enough money to cover your expenses. The amount varies by your personal situation and whether you live with your parents or are self-sufficient. These loans don't have to be repaid until after you graduate. The key thing to look for is that the loan is "subsidized," which means the federal government will make the interest payments while you are in college (and for the first 6 months after graduation). Stafford Loans have repayment periods of up to 25 years, depending on the total amount you borrow throughout your college career.

Another loan is the federal Parent PLUS loan and is actually a loan that is made to the parent(s) for the student's college costs.

These loans, if they're offered, will be described in material that comes from the college you will attend. Pay careful attention to the loan details, and research the repayment terms before signing anything.

Scholarship Spotlight

There are scholarships available by participating in online quizzes. These quizzes are formatted in tournament fashion and there is no entry fee. There are different categories, depending on the applicant's age and school status (Common Knowledge Scholarship Foundation, 2009). For more details, visit http://www.cksf.org.

What's Your Major?

4

It's a Common Question

WE hear it in movies all the time. Two college students meet and the shy boy wants to strike up a conversation with the girl. Unable to come up with something more original, he asks, "What's your major?"

Now, although it's a good question, it's one freshmen get asked hundreds of time, so it's not going to make much of a first impression if you have romance on your mind.

But this is a book about finding college funding—and winning it—and so it's one of the first questions you need to think about as you begin your search for scholarship money. Why is it important? There are some obvious reasons, of course. If you're going to major in mathematics, you probably won't want to waste your time applying for journalism scholarships. One of the things you'll be looking at is your major's program at various colleges.

For example, there are a lot of institutional scholarships out there. These scholarships often are disbursed through departments in the college, or schools within a university system.

The point here is that your major will dictate which department or school you'll be entered in. And that will qualify you for particular institutional scholarships. It's a good idea to understand the availability of these institutional scholarships as you consider what to major in at school.

Scholarship Spotlight

The Ayn Rand Institute has three categories of essay contests for scholarship money. The categories are based on grade level for middle and high school students. College students also may enter. There are 534 awards available that add up to $85,000 in prize money (Ayn Rand Foundation, 2009). For more details, visit http://www.aynrand.org.

Fine Tuning

We hope that you've purchased a notebook and started a journal, your process of self-evaluation. If you've done so, you'll have thought about your skill sets and what sort of careers you're interested in.

Now it's time to fine tune the process. If you've made up your mind already and have a specific career decided on, good for you. But you still might want to read on. It could give you some ideas you haven't yet considered.

Some Considerations

When declaring your major, ask about the possibilities of switching majors later in your academic career. There are some programs that are fairly rigid in prerequisite courses. A prerequisite course is one that is required before you can move on to the next course in the program.

For example, Scott declared his major as physics. He considered switching majors and going into one of the engineering programs. Luckily, many of the prerequisite courses for physics were the same for the sophomore-level engineering classes. He would have had to take a freshman engineering course, though, and that would have set back his graduation date by a semester. (If you're going into the humanities, you might have more flexibility to change majors while attending college.)

It's not just the time involved, either, in switching majors and extending the traditional 4-year college degree program. It's the expense. Adding those extra classes and semesters mean paying extra tuition. Another thing to consider when delaying the graduation date is delaying employment and earning a paycheck. The end game here is to get a career, and a semester or two delay in getting a degree is a semester or two delay in earning a salary.

Speaking of careers, author and college planning expert Sandra L. Berger (2006) suggested that arranging a meeting with a coordinator at the college's career center can help high school students plan their college journey.

Cash Clue

A major doesn't necessarily define your career. For example, a degree in biology can lead to a job that is related to environmental protection.

Journal

You're continuing to write in your journal, right? Here's a topic for your journal. Examine your motives for attending college. For some people, going to college after high school is simply an automatic assumption. Everyone *expects* you to go to college, so you sign up, go through the motions, then find yourself as a freshman in a school and start scratching your head, wondering,

"Why am I here?" Well, if you examine ahead of time why you're going, then you'll know the answer to this question.

Having this knowledge also will help with the motivation to pass your courses. Knowing you want a specific degree and want to work in a specific field, you'll have a self-given reason for studying. And there will be long nights of study. That's what happens at college.

A Note About College

We're not here to criticize high schools. We've known many wonderful teachers, and in our case, our children got great educations. But there's always room for improvement, right? And if we had to single out an aspect of high school that we believe could be improved, it would be the teaching of study habits.

Scott went off to NCSSM and learned how to study while in high school, but our other children didn't receive that kind of detail. Studying is something that needs to be practiced before heading off to college.

Doug remembers when he showed up at college. On his first day, when he met his roommate, he was astonished to find that his roommate had already purchased all of the textbooks required for his first semester courses. Not only that, his roommate had already read them!

The roommate explained that he didn't study them, per se, but he had found that reading class material ahead of time helped him to listen closer to what the teacher was saying in class. Otherwise, he would have to spend most of his class time writing notes, and he thought this didn't help with long-term understanding of the material. The roommate went on to be accepted into medical school in his junior year of undergraduate work.

So, take some time to practice studying. Read material ahead of time. Don't wait until the last minute to start on assignments. These all sound like simple hints, and they're easily dismissed.

WHAT'S YOUR MAJOR? | **49**

After all, many high school students who have achieved academically don't really need to do a lot of homework to make good grades. High school doesn't present enough of a challenge to these students, and they find themselves somewhat at a loss when they go to college. They might find themselves swamped halfway through the first semester. Don't make that mistake. Stay ahead of the game by practicing good study habits.

Wait, I Want to Do Something Else

So, you're writing in your journal and realize that you simply want a career in law enforcement. You're not interested in being a detective or some other official that might require a 4-year degree. You want to start working on the streets.

You might not need a 4-year degree. You might be able to get your degree at a community college, ensuring your employment. This is what happened with Thomas.

Of course, the cost of a 2-year degree is much less than going to college for 4 years. And Thomas figured he would be making an income for 2 years when, if he'd chosen a 4-year school, he would be paying for tuition for his junior and senior years. That's a net difference of tens of thousands of dollars. We're not suggesting that money should be the primary consideration when choosing this 2-year route, but if you're thinking about fine-tuning your major and discover that an associate's degree will get you where you're going, then there can be a financial benefit.

Yes, we know the argument about long-term earning potential with bachelor's degrees. It's a statistical truth. The higher your academic degree, the more earnings you'll make in your adult life. But we like to think that other factors such as job satisfaction should be considered. Also, any money that you make in those 2 years that would have otherwise gone into schooling can be put into savings and draw interest (or some other safe investment) and be earning that interest for years before a 4-year student graduates. Know, too, that some employers will pay you to continue your education, so you could get hired with a 2-year degree, then work toward the 4-year degree.

Employment Opportunities

Let's say you've done a good job with your journal and you know your interests inside and out. You have a firm grasp of your skill sets. You know what you're good at and what you're not so enthusiastic about.

Let's say you're really interested in the study of history.

We're not going to stand here and try to dissuade you from following your passion. We remember some fantastic novels in which the main character's profession was the teaching of history. And if anyone has seen the movie character Indiana Jones, remember that he teaches archeology. But if you look through the want ads or browse through career websites such as http://www.monster.com, you're simply not going to find many postings seeking history or archeology majors. By the way, we encourage you to look through the Monster website, along with any other employment website you can find, and get a feel for what kind of jobs are plentiful (if any). Sometimes the job market is tough, and in a recession, many employers cut back.

We want to make two points here.

One is that if you're going to major in a subject like archeology or history, strongly consider having teaching as a minor. This will allow you to have the option of teaching the subject that you're so interested in. And it'll leave open some employment opportunities upon graduation.

The second point is that when fine-tuning your decision of majors one consideration is employment potential. We would hate to see someone declare a history major by default. That is, no other major leaped off the page as something of great interest, and so history was chosen because it was relatively easy to learn and a lot of prerequisite courses are standard courses taken by most freshman students.

Cash Clue

Remember that you'll do best in a major in which you have a lot of interest. Hopefully your talents will match these, but place emphasis on your interest in a particular field.

Case Study of How Not to Declare a Major

One of the reasons we were so focused on helping our children explore their interests and themselves in order to find out what their majors should be is because of what happened to Doug.

Doug always wanted to be a writer. He knew it from seventh grade. But not just a writer. If that was his goal, he would have majored in journalism or English. That would have set him up nicely to work as a newspaper writer or in some facet of the publishing business, perhaps as a copy writer.

No, Doug wanted to write novels, but knew that it would require years and years of writing before he would meet with success. It's no secret that very few people make a living at writing novels. It's a brutal business, and even fairly successful novel writers aren't rich.

So, Doug chose a major by selecting what came most easily to him and what looked like a career in which there were plenty of opportunities.

He chose chemistry. OK, it's not the favorite subject of many, perhaps most, high school students, but Doug loved it. It came easily to him because his mind works in a very analytic manner, and everything in chemistry was logical and orderly and followed sets of rules. Doug did fine for 2 years at college, but then when he started getting into the courses that required a greater degree of dedication, he discovered he simply wasn't all that interested in it. He wanted to write, after all, not stand in a lab and pour liquids of different colors into beakers and measure the thermal response.

Doug didn't make it through with a chemistry major. But he didn't give up. He decided that majoring in engineering was a better way to go. He switched colleges and declared chemical engineering as his major. After a year of that, with tuition bills piling up and no closer to a degree, he decided to enlist in the military and let them pay for an electronics education.

That worked out nicely for him, and he worked in the electronics field after his 4-year military tour was up. The military enlistment also allowed him to pay his educational debt. We're not suggesting anyone join the military solely for the purpose of getting a free education, but it's an option Doug chose and it worked for him.

By the way, 20 years after dropping out of school, while working in the electronics industry, Doug went back to get his degree. He majored in mathematics, a great major for someone with an analytical mind like his. He didn't pursue employment in a mathematical field, but earning a degree always looks good on a resume. And besides, he hated to think of all of those semester hours going to waste. Now at least he has a diploma to show for all his hard work, and he went on to earn a master's degree.

College Costs

As we've pointed out, the cost of going to school for an associate's degree at a community college is a lot less than going to a 4-year private college. In general, private colleges are going to cost more than public universities because the public universities receive government assistance. The private colleges have to make the financial balance sheets work without that government help.

On the other hand, here's an important consideration. The more expensive the school, the greater your financial need, and the more scholarship money you'll be eligible for. We'll go into more details about this in the next chapter, where we discuss actually picking your school. But for now, don't let the cost of a college deter you from selecting the college and major that's best for you For example, there are some colleges that have great programs in anthropology. You're not likely to get an associate's degree that will qualify you for employment in that field. That's fine.

But when you're making notes in your journal, finding out what interests you, keep an open mind. For most people, these decisions aren't black and white. We're human beings, after all, and we're full of self-contradictions and shades of gray. We tend to lean in one direction or another without that shining, guiding light of surety that we all pray for from time to time.

If that's the case, you'll want to note what majors interest you, even if they're not your primary considerations. The reason? We might find that when we investigate colleges in the next chapter, there are facets about those majors that fascinate you. And there might be career opportunities that you haven't discovered yet.

Cash Clue

Read through your journal from time to time. Past journal entries might point you to something you've forgotten, such as that spark you felt when you learned something about global warming in science class.

The Right Way to Declare a Major—A Case Study

Our son Alan had it right when he declared music as his major. He also will have education as a minor so that he will be able to teach music after he graduates.

But, his selection of a major allowed him to fine-tune his choice while he's in school. He is still writing in his journal, and he engages us from time to time in discussions about where he's going with his college education.

It goes back to that absence of the shining beacon of light showing him (and us) the way. We don't have concrete answers for him, but we've found that by asking him questions, we can help him explore his feelings about college and his major, and this will help him to determine if he wants to switch majors within the music department.

His major will remain related to music. We all know that much. But he might angle more to a performance major than an education aspect. That is, there are majors he could declare with which he would be more qualified to obtain employment as a studio musician.

Not being familiar with employment opportunities in the field of music, we did some online investigation and discovered that there are job opportunities for studio musicians. Other musicians are employed in theaters, such as those on Broadway, in which musicals are performed.

The point we're trying to make here is that for Alan, the process of fine-tuning his major is continuing in his freshman year of college. For many degree programs, this is perfectly acceptable. Colleges want you to be in the major that will interest you the most because they understand it will increase your motivation and will tend to keep you enrolled.

Alan plays the trombone. One evening, he called us into the living room, where he was watching television. "Look!" he said. "That is what I want to do!"

There was a musical show on. One band had just finished playing on stage, and the next act had been announced. As we watched, two people rode a motorcycle onto the stage. The rider in back was holding a trombone. As the motorcycle stopped center stage, the man in back raised the trombone to his lips and began playing. A few moments later, his backup band joined in.

Well, we were thusly enlightened! Alan wants to perform, but not in any usual way. He wants to blaze his own performance path. We think it's great that he has a vision and is pursuing it. But he understands, too, that the day after he graduates will not bring a performing contract that will set him up financially for life. (Actually, we don't think the day after graduation brings that for anyone. We are a performance-based society, after all.)

We encourage him (and you!) to pursue your dreams, whether on motorcycle or not, but keep in mind that you'll eventually need a day job when fine-tuning your college major.

Dealing With Uncertainty

Some people are able to roll with the punches more easily than others. They don't seem to mind at all that they have an undeclared major. It doesn't affect them that the time is counting down when a firm decision will have to be made. These people tend to think that things will work themselves out. And who knows, maybe for them it does.

But for others, uncertainty can be a nagging, frustrating feeling that not only detracts from the college experience, but also can be a drag on grades and a factor in a student dropping out of college. Uncertainty can lead to paralysis of thought and action, not good for college students on whom there are many demands. And so we've tried to instill a few coping mechanisms in our children for dealing with uncertainty.

By the way, there will come a day when uncertainty reaches monumental levels in the life of a college student. And that will be as graduation day approaches. Even if a student has a job lined up, heading out into the real world is the epitome of uncertainty. These students don't know what daily life will be like. What will the job be like? Will he like his coworkers? Or maybe the student is fretting about the possibility of going to graduate school.

Lynn is going through a troubled period now. She doesn't have a job lined up yet, and graduation day is only months away, but with her credentials, winning a teaching fellowship among other resume highlights, she's sure to land a job. But where? The only stipulation her teaching fellowship has is that she teach in the state of North Carolina. She's talked about finding someplace close to the coast, so that she can enjoy her weekends by spending them on a beach, basking in the sun. Sounds good! But she's also interested in living closer to a big city like Raleigh or Charlotte.

So how can you handle the uncertainty when you haven't even decided on your major? By writing in your journal, knowing you're doing all you can to stay on top of things. After all, ask yourself the question, "Am I doing everything I can to ensure my future is the one I think is best for myself?" If the answer is yes, then there's no more you can do. You have to let things play out. Yes, there's uncertainty in it, but you have to realize that there will always be positive aspects to change. There will be negative ones, too. Nobody that we know of has a string of positives that continues throughout a lifetime. Good luck with that! Seriously, do what you can and then know you've done your homework and you'll have enough confidence to deal with new situations as they arise.

You've made it through college, we tell Lynn, so you can deal with whatever the world throws at you. You can always talk to your parents, and we encourage you to share your feelings with as many of your friends as possible, because this will lead you to feel like you have a good understanding of the situation and yourself, even if there's a degree of uncertainty involved.

Take a Tour

We have a chapter in this book in which we'll go into depth on where to go online to find scholarship money. But for now, we want to mention one place you can look—the college website. This can help you with your self-examination about choosing a college major and how that will affect scholarship opportunities.

Use your search engine to find the website of the college

you're thinking of attending. You can also try a virtual tour website such as http://www.campustours.com. Search the website (or the campus, virtually) and pay particular attention to the departments and majors offered. Note any mention of financial aid and whom to contact for more information about financial aid. There usually is an e-mail address you can use to contact the financial aid office. Be honest and ask questions. You will receive information that might be able to help you fine-tune your major.

Cash Clue

Doctors and lawyers generally make a lot of money, but do you know what other professions earn? Keep in mind as you search online those occupations that are more exotic, such as careers in forensics, gaming design, and virtual marketing. Consider finding a niche career that will have employers begging at your feet.

A Final Note on Scholarships and Majors

When fine-tuning your major, don't forget about new scholarship opportunities that could arise.

Talk with the professors and the financial aid department of your college. See if there is any additional scholarship money available from the college for different majors. Look online, too. We'll show you in a later chapter how to hunt online for scholarship money, but for now, just keep in mind that a declared major will qualify you for some particular scholarships and disqualify you from others.

If you're interested in funding your education for free, keep examining your major throughout your academic career and find the scholarship opportunities that open and close with any change you make.

Scholarship Spotlight

There are 10 scholarships offered annually by the American Fire Sprinkler Association. After reading an essay, applicants are simply required to take a 10-question open-book quiz. Each scholarship is for $2,000 (American Fire Sprinkler Association, 2009). For more details, visit http://www. afsascholarship.org.

Choosing a College

The A in GRAND SLAM

ANALYZE the match between you and the college. We've already talked a little about choosing a college. We'll go into that process in more detail throughout this chapter as well as give you some tips on how choosing a college affects your scholarship opportunities.

Scholarship Spotlight

The Eastman Scholarship Foundation awards scholarships to students in the fields of cinematography and film, including film production. Awards vary from $1,000 to $5,000. Film submissions are judged on visual imagery, creative ability, and other criteria ("Kodak," 2009). For more details, visit http://motion.kodak.com/US/en/motion/Education/Discounts_And_Scholarships/index.htm.

Case in Point

Want to hear about an instant scholarship offer we received from a small private college in Virginia? We investigated, of course, before responding with any personal information. There are unscrupulous people out there fishing for personal information. Identity theft is a real danger for people searching for scholarships because many of the scholarship search engines need your personal profile to tailor the search. Students can get into the habit of answering personal information questions without thinking.

But this was a real deal, a scholarship offer of around $15,000 per year for Lynn. When we researched the cost of the private college, however, we found that the tuition was about $30,000 per year. That would leave Lynn with a cost greater than the tuition at an in-state public university. We advised Lynn to decline, but she wasn't interested in attending that particular Virginia college anyway, so it was a moot offer.

Still, this taught us an important point. The costs associated with a particular college can affect the amount of the scholarship. Generally, the greater the cost of a college, the greater the amount of the scholarship. This makes sense when you remember that your family's financial contribution is assumed to be a constant, regardless of the cost of a college. If the family contribution remains the same and the cost of the education rises, the financial need rises. And scholarships (at least many of them) are affected by financial need.

Cash Clue
College admission applications cost money. Check to see what the fees are before deciding on how many colleges to apply for admission.

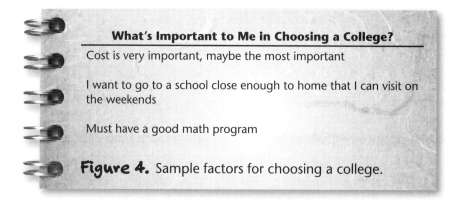

What's Important to Me in Choosing a College?

Cost is very important, maybe the most important

I want to go to a school close enough to home that I can visit on the weekends

Must have a good math program

Figure 4. Sample factors for choosing a college.

The Questions

When deciding on a college, there are questions you need to ask yourself. Journal time! We know we keep stressing writing in your journal, but when you use a journal to help yourself choose a college, you'll be able to look back at your decision and understand why you made it. You won't be one of those students who wonder, "Why did I ever come to this campus?"

So ask yourself if you want to choose a college that is the best for your chosen major and career. Or, would you prefer to go to a college that is the most affordable because of your financial situation? Or maybe you want to go a college close to home. Make another list, like the one in Figure 4, this time asking "What's important to me in choosing a college?"

Remember, though, that going to a college that is more expensive than others usually will result in more scholarship opportunities, so just because it's expensive, don't assume you can't afford to go there.

These questions generally will narrow down your choices. And once you narrow down your choices, it's time to get more information about the remaining candidates. Of course, if you're having trouble narrowing down your field, you can always use the information-gathering techniques we're going to talk about. It's just more time-consuming when you have a large list of colleges to investigate.

Questions for Thomas

For Thomas, his questions were relatively basic. He knew what he wanted in a career—to go into law enforcement. This was based on his experience in the U.S. Marine Corps. He liked the discipline and professionalism that a law enforcement career would provide.

Because Thomas already had a family, his primary question was finding a college near his home. He needed to spend time with his family, and a long commute was out of the question. Going off and living on campus was not a consideration at all.

A brief investigation revealed that all of the nearby criminal justice degree programs offered about the same benefits as far as placement services go. Because his educational expenses were limited by what the G.I. Bill would pay, he enrolled in the nearest, most affordable college, allowing him a larger amount of leftover G.I. Bill money for a living expenses stipend. Thomas also selected a college that offered night courses. It was a community college, and many of its graduates were hired soon after graduation. Perfect!

Cash Clue

When you're investigating a college, talk to the career placement department. You can do this by phone or e-mail. Ask about the percentage of graduating seniors finding employment. If 99% of graduates are getting jobs, the chances are good that the program is seen in a good light by the hiring community.

Questions for Grace

Grace's main questions revolved around how to get the education she needed for the career she wanted in photography. Although there were college programs that would prepare her for such a career, she was very cost conscious. Grace also had a family, and therefore she looked close to home.

During her search, she stumbled upon an internship program. Although it would not give her the degree credentials that a college could offer, the internship program existed locally. And not only that, she could earn a salary while learning her craft. Her financial need probably would have resulted in many scholarship opportunities, but she chose the internship route, taking curriculum classes in the evening for specialized subjects.

Questions for Lynn

Lynn wanted a college that had a good teacher preparation program. Although this was her primary concern, cost was another factor. And for anyone reading a book about how to fund a college education, we're guessing it's a factor for you, too.

Lynn also wanted to live near home, even though she would be staying on campus. Still, this led her to the same choice, because the nearest university was also the one with the great reputation for educating teachers-to-be.

When the scholarship package came in from this college, the deal was sealed, and that's the college she attended.

Questions for Scott

Scott had a little more difficult time than our other children. Because he spent the last 2 years of high school at a boarding school, there was no intimidation factor for moving far away from home. On the other hand, he didn't have a clear-cut career goal. The fact that Lynn wanted to be a teacher guided her directly to a choice of college, but this would not work for Scott.

Because he generally knew he would want to find employment in a discipline that was related to science (with a heavy dose of mathematics if possible), he decided that he would need to go to a college that offered a wide variety of choices of major within the sphere of scientific interests.

Although many other colleges offered excellent degree programs in narrow fields, there was one college that stood out with its engineering and science programs that are quite wide-ranging.

But Scott had a second issue. His girlfriend was attending a college that was a 2-hour drive away. Scott considered attending a college closer to her, but in the end, the excellence of the programs offered by his school of choice won out. During his sophomore year, his girlfriend transferred to the college he is still attending. She is doing quite well there, although she is not interested in majoring in anything related to science. But that's a benefit of a large school. It can have programs that are of interest to anyone.

Questions for Alan

Alan wanted to attend a college that had a good music program, as well as excellent programs in the humanities.

Normally, that would have led him directly to the college that Lynn chose. But this is where deciding on a school can be affected by other factors.

The last of our five children, Alan was very conscious of wanting to blaze his own trail. Imagine attending a high school in which all of the teachers, coaches, and counselors first greet you with conversation about your older siblings and what wonderful students they were. And then follow this up with their continued talk about your siblings, asking how they're doing.

In such a situation, it would be very understandable for a teenager to want to go to a college farther away from home. Such a student might want to establish a degree of independence, and this is exactly what Alan did. He chose the program that fit his educational needs and was about as far away from home as possible where he could still get in-state tuition rates.

Virtual Tours

We mentioned taking a virtual tour during your quest to decide on a career (at least preliminarily). Now it's time to reexamine the virtual tour as you're choosing a college. You can visit a virtual tour website such as http://www.campustours.com and tour the college campus of your choice. Remember that many colleges also have virtual tour links on their websites. Simply type the name of the college you're considering into an Internet search engine if you don't know the college's website URL.

Cash Clue

Remember that colleges are going to show their best aspects during a virtual tour. It's not that the tours can be misleading, but they will certainly leave out anything that might give a bad impression.

Other Information Sources

We encourage you to find out as much as you can about the colleges on your short list.

✓ Get in touch with the career placement office. See what kind of success they've had with helping graduating seniors find employment.
✓ Find out what the dropout rate is for incoming freshman.
✓ Find out what kind of clubs and extracurricular activities the college offers.

You can find much of this information on the college's website, but we think that calling the college and talking to people who work there can give you a more thorough understanding of the information. In other words, the website might tell you about the apple, but talking to people will let you know that the apples are delicious.

You also can go to a library and find books that describe different colleges. We've been known to browse through a few of these books at a bookstore without actually purchasing the book. And if there are only a couple of colleges you want to look at, you might need only a few minutes of browsing.

If you're worried about crime, you can conduct research to find out what the crime rates are in the college's city and county.

Cash Clue

If you go to a library or bookstore to browse through one of the college guidebooks, take a pen and notepad to take notes. You might think you can remember the pertinent information, but it always pays to write it down. You can transfer the information to a journal when you get back home.

Of course, nothing beats actually visiting the campus. You can look at pictures online, stroll the quad in a virtual world, and read quotes from alumni, but you won't get the actual feel of the campus unless you visit it. If it's a long drive from your home, you can find an inexpensive hotel nearby so that you don't feel rushed. Call the admissions office to arrange for a tour. Generally, colleges will schedule campus tours for groups of potential incoming freshmen, so call early and add your name to the list. If you can't make one of these group tours, you can usually arrange for a mini-tour with the admissions office. And if they can't arrange one, take a tour by yourself. You can walk the campus and talk to the students there. Make sure you have some questions ready. You might want to consider asking students what they like best about the college and what its biggest drawback is.

Other Factors

We've mentioned factors that will affect your decision on which college to attend, and we'd like to take another look at these factors. Get out your journal when you're considering a college and look at that college in relation to the following:
- ✓ distance from family and friends,
- ✓ the fit with your career and major choices,
- ✓ the cost of the college,

✓ the size of the college,
✓ perks a college offers,
✓ college reputation and graduate degree considerations, and
✓ dropout rates.

Distance From Family and Friends

Some students want to get as far away from family as possible. When you consider that tuition often is higher for out-of-state students, the distance can be limited. Remember our son Alan? He took this route and ended up a 5-hour drive away. This turned out to be far enough, because for a family member to visit on a day trip, he or she was looking at a total drive time of 10 hours.

Other students want to stay near home for moral support (and maybe to bring the laundry home on the weekends). Our daughter Lynn fit into this category, which worked out fine because the college she really liked also was near home.

Get out your journal and write down your thoughts about the points that follow. Remember to be honest with yourself. There are no right answers. You simply want to make the best choice of college for yourself.

If you're thinking about a college far from home, consider the following:

✓ You might miss your friends and family and find yourself feeling lonely.
✓ You will not have family support "right around the corner" for any kind of emergency you have.
✓ Coming home for the holidays and on breaks will be more of a headache.
✓ It will take more time to acclimate to your new surroundings.

Here are some considerations if you're looking at a college near your home:

✓ Your lifestyle might have interference from family and friends.

✓ You might not have the same opportunity to gain a sense of independence.

✓ You might be choosing geography over quality of college.

Fit With Career and Major Choices

Most colleges have areas in which they excel, as we've already discussed. These colleges have built reputations that can be valuable upon graduating from college. For example, if you're interested in engineering, a liberal arts college is probably not the best fit for you.

Take out your journal and write down a list of pros and cons for "Fit With Major" and use this in your evaluation of choosing a college.

Cost of the College

Cost is always a consideration. If you evaluate two colleges as being equal in everything other than cost, then by all means go with the less expensive one. But chances are, you will have to weigh cost versus other factors. Perhaps you want to live close to home, but the closer colleges are more expensive. It's like a balancing act. You can make the decision clearer with lists of pros and cons.

Remember to keep in mind that a more expensive college will probably offer more financial aid. You might have to wait to make a decision about cost until you see what kind of institutional financial aid a college offers you.

Size of the College

Smaller colleges generally are believed to have atmospheres that are cozier than larger universities. Most of the buildings on the campuses of small colleges are within easy walking distance. There's a sense of togetherness in the student body. Some larger colleges can make students feel like numbers, getting lost in the crowds.

Smaller colleges tend to have smaller class sizes, and you'll find professors who know you by name. They might even greet you as you walk along the quad. Larger universities have large student bodies, and it's more difficult to make that one-on-one connection with the faculty.

There are, of course, advantages to larger universities. They tend to have a larger list of potential majors. If you're sure of your major, fine. But if you think you might switch majors, or if you have no clear idea, then a larger university will have more options for you down the road.

Cash Clue

When our son Alan was finishing his first year of college, he decided to transfer to his second choice (initially) school, which was closer to home. The distance from home wasn't the deciding factor, though. It was the college atmosphere. Alan found out that most of the student body at his first school went home on the weekends, leaving only those students who wanted to party all weekend. Because Alan wanted an atmosphere that was more serious about learning, this was not the right college for him.

Perks a College Offers

Make sure you read through the college catalogs, browse the college website, and call the admissions office to find out any specific perks that the college offers. For example, we know of a small liberal arts college that vigorously promotes foreign study. Because of alumni donations, the semester of foreign study costs no more than a semester on campus. What a great perk!

Cash Clue

A semester of foreign study can be invaluable in helping a student become well rounded and develop a deeper understanding of the world.

College Reputation and Graduate Study Considerations

If you have any aspirations of going on to graduate school for a master's or doctoral degree, ask about acceptance rates into graduate schools from the college you're considering. For example, going to Harvard as an undergraduate boosts (quite a bit!) your chances of being accepted into graduate school. It's difficult sometimes to gauge the reputation of a college within the business and academic community. There are books that grade colleges, and they're probably pretty good at generally listing colleges near the top and colleges near the bottom, but we wouldn't advise taking them as gospel. For example, a college might not be ranked high overall, but might have an outstanding theatre program.

When you investigate a college's reputation in the business and academic community, it helps if you're looking at a specific major, especially within larger universities, because they can vary widely from department to department.

Cash Clue

Some colleges offer extensive work-study programs. Ask about them. Not only can you earn a few extra bucks, the experience will be great on your resume when you graduate and begin looking for a job.

We found that, as a general rule, the higher the entrance requirements for a college, the better its reputation in the community. This makes sense, because if the academic quality of the incoming freshmen is high, there generally is a higher degree of academic rigor at the college. This isn't always true, and it's also helpful to look at the entrance requirements for specific degree programs at the college.

Dropout Rates

When you contact a college, ask what the dropout rates. If it has a high dropout rate, you have to ask yourself, why? Make sure to include this fact in your list of pros and cons. Keep in mind, though, there are many reasons that students dropout of college. The first semester always has the highest dropout rate, mostly due to culture shock from the student being away from home and homesickness.

Cash Clue

Don't let homesickness ruin your college experience. Get through the first semester, then worry about homesickness later. It will pass. In the meantime, use e-mails, visits, online video chatting, and phone calls to keep in close touch with home.

The Master Pro/Con List

For each question you ask yourself, you might find that one college had advantages over another. In this vein, you can make a pro/con list for each factor. For example, if one of your colleges has a very low dropout rate, you could list that as a pro for that college. After you examine the questions for each school by writing in your journal, combine your pro/con lists into one big list (see Figure 5).

But what will you do with this list? Stare at it? Sometimes, after we've done all the work, we're mentally exhausted with the lists. That's when it's time to take the list and talk about your college choices with friends and family and anyone you know that might

	College A	College B	College C
Near home	pro	pro	con
Fit with major	con	con	pro
College size	pro	con	pro

Figure 5. Master pro/con list for choosing colleges.

have something to say about it. Don't do this in a single day. Talk about your list over a period of days or maybe weeks if you're ahead of the game with regard to time.

Then you can narrow down your list to the college that is best for you, based on your discussions. At the very least you should be able to narrow down your list to a workable number, say around three. If you pick more than three, you won't be able to focus on making a decision.

Even if you do narrow down the list to the best college available, keep a second and third choice on your list of colleges. You might not get admitted into the college of your choice, and you want to have a backup choice (or two).

Once you've narrowed your choices down, it's time to move on to other things like scholarships and financial aid. And as you move down the road, there will be things that happen that will sway you to one school or another. Based on our experience, this happens more often than not.

More Factors to Consider

Now that you've examined the questions that are important to you when deciding on a college, we'd like to throw a few more factors at you that you might not have considered. If you've already considered these factors, great! If not, these might help you to reach a decision. Regardless, these factors will help you to understand what kind of college campus you'll be spending time on. We didn't list them yet because they're a bit more difficult to gauge.

For the factors remaining in this chapter, go back to your journal and make a pro/con list for each. We'll help you along with our opinions on what a pro and what a con is for each. But you might feel differently, so be true to yourself, your gut feeling, about each.

College Atmosphere

Regardless of size, some colleges have reputations of being party schools. Go back over your research and see if you can find information about the campus atmosphere. If needed, you can contact the college and ask to speak to an admissions counselor. Ask questions about the atmosphere of the school. Of course, they will tell you that the students are serious about their academic work, but you can sometimes get useful information, and sometimes they'll admit there is a reputation but will explain why it's not relevant.

One good method of finding out about the atmosphere is to search for online forums for a particular school and read what the students have to say.

Sometimes you can gauge a college campus better on a weekday and sometimes on the weekends. This turned out to be the case for Alan. He visited his campus during the week, and he found that the students there were serious about achieving academic success. Then the weekends came. As it turns out, most of the students went home on the weekends. The college was in a remote area of North Carolina, and this likely was a factor for the students who wanted to leave the campus on the weekends.

But the problem for Alan was that the students who remained on campus during the weekends took that time to throw parties. He grew frustrated at not being able to find study partners and a peaceful atmosphere on the weekends. This fact alone soured him on the college, and he has since transferred.

Rural Versus Big City

There are small colleges in big cities and small colleges that are more distant from cities. Although freshmen generally will be spending much of their time on campus, there will be limitations on living off campus in later years if the college is in a rural setting. However, for students interested in nature and who enjoy outdoor activities, a rural setting can be a real plus. For example, our son Alan was only minutes away from off-road bike trails and rivers with plenty of access points for canoes. The same simply can't be said for a college in New York City. On the other hand, there are plenty of opportunities for cultural activities for students attending a college in New York or another large city, opportunities that weren't available for Alan.

Note that most small colleges have programs in which artists visit campus for lectures or to serve as professors. Just because a college is in a rural setting, it doesn't mean that it's cut off completely from the outside world. If this is a concern of yours, talk to the admissions office and ask about cultural events the college sponsors.

Liberal Arts Colleges

Cash Clue

We believe that part of a college education should include elements of a liberal arts education. This helps students become more well rounded and thus helps to prepare them for life in the "real world." However, a liberal arts education alone might not be especially beneficial when looking for employment. Be sure you understand the employment potential for your chosen degree.

Some colleges have excellent reputations as liberal arts colleges. We've found that many of these are great for students who want to pursue higher degrees. Just as colleges look for incoming students who are well rounded, graduate degree programs look for the same thing, although perhaps not to the same degree.

Some colleges, such as technical colleges, are more focused on specific disciplines, usually on an education in preparation for a specific career.

When you examine the colleges you're thinking about attending, ask students and faculty to rate the college as a place for a liberal arts education. And then evaluate how a liberal arts education fits in with your career goals.

Scholarship Spotlight

The Society of Vacuum Coaters offers scholarships to students interested in the technology of vacuum coating. In addition to demonstrating financial need, applicants should have an interest in the study of vacuum coating and have good grades (SVC Foundation, 2009). For more details, visit http://www.svc.org.

Finding Information

The N in GRAND SLAM

NAVIGATE your way to scholarship money.

In this chapter we'll show you how we used the Internet and other sources to find scholarship money and apply for it. With millions and millions of dollars of scholarship money available, just waiting for your application, the problem isn't that scholarship money isn't out there, the problem is finding it. And then writing a terrific application and winning that scholarship.

Although there are local scholarships available, many of which can be found at your high school counseling office, there is a vast wealth of scholarship money that can be applied for online. That's why we're here to show you how to navigate your way to the sources of scholarship money.

Scholarship Spotlight

The Association of Firearm and Tool Mark Examiners awards $1,000 scholarships to students who plan to pursue careers in forensic science. These scholarships do not automatically renew each year; new applications must be submitted. These are merit-based scholarships (Association of Firearm and Tool Mark Examiners, 2009). For more details, visit http://www.afte.org/AssociationInfo/a_scholarship.htm.

The Secret: Have a System

We suppose it's not a unique secret. That is, other people have systems. The key for us, though, was to have a system and stick to it.

Why do you need a system when you approach the task of finding scholarship money? In case you haven't started looking yet, you might not know. If you have done some searching, then you probably already know. It's too easy to get lost in the vastness of the Internet, in the complications of application processes. You'll spend hour after hour hunting and reading, only to find that you're not eligible. It's too easy to throw your hands in the air and give up.

Our method of navigating the Internet and searching for scholarships will save you time and keep up your motivation. Our system won't give you any quick money. Applications take time to process. But with our system, you can track your progress. And perhaps more importantly, you'll know that you're making progress. There's nothing that takes the wind out of sails more quickly than feeling like you're wasting your time.

The First Search

Remember those math classes in high school that taught you a method to solve math problems, the old method, even though there's a timesaving, quick way to solve the problem? The math teacher would say that knowing how to solve the problem the hard way would help students understand the nature of the problem.

In the same way, we're going to give you a challenge. This is how we started our search for scholarship money for our children.

It startled us that we could waste so much time looking for scholarships. We think everyone should experience the long way of searching for scholarships and the easy way. Not that solving math problems the long way is a waste of time (Doug majored in math, remember), but it does teach an appreciation of having a method to solve a problem, even if that problem is finding scholarship money.

Go to your favorite Internet search engine and type in the words "scholarship money." Many search engines have paid search results (sponsored results), and we suggest that you avoid those. After all, they are from companies that have paid the search engine to show up high in the search engine results when a particular set of words is typed into the search field—in this case, scholarship money. For us, this means that they have something to sell you so that they can recoup their investment in sponsoring the search term. You shouldn't have to spend a dime in your search for scholarship money. If you ever get tempted, remember that for scholarships, money flows *toward* the student.

After you see your results, check the time and write it down. We're going to see just how much time you need to search the top five websites that showed up in your search.

Now that you've recorded the time, click on the top result. Read through the information there and try to find out how to apply for a scholarship. You're going to have to fill out a form, perhaps, or enter your personal information. Do this one item at a time, as though you haven't read this book and have a file handy that has all of the information available for copying and pasting into forms. Repeat the above procedure for the next four websites on your search for scholarship money.

After you're finished, if you've had the patience to work your way through all of them, check the time again and see how many hours you've spent. Do you feel frustrated? Have you wasted your time? We don't think it was a waste. It's a good introduction to the world of scholarship searches.

Our Method

We'll go into more detail about some of these steps in later chapters, but the search for scholarships on the Internet can be boiled down to the following:

1. Schedule a set amount of time per week and a specific time of the week for scholarship searches.
2. Keep a file with your pertinent personal and financial information so you can copy and paste it into forms and applications.
3. Create a new e-mail account specifically for scholarship application purposes.
4. Record the scholarship names that you apply for, including application deadlines and dates the scholarship winners are notified.
5. Make notes for promising scholarships to check later as you conduct your searches so you don't get sidetracked.
6. Follow up immediately on any request for additional information.
7. Keep going.

Simple enough? Sure, it's a simple method, but simple methods work. Ask any coach about the importance of fundamentals in sports competitions. The coach can tell you that the team that can't play with sound fundamentals is the team that won't win the game or match.

Expanding Your Search

When searching the Internet for scholarships using a search engine such as Google or Yahoo, try typing in the word "scholarship" with words that apply to you but not other potential scholarship applicants. For example, try the county in which you live: *Macomb County scholarship*. We suggest the state in which you live. *Texas scholarship*. You also can try: *Texas college scholarship*. Are you left handed? Try typing in *scholarships for left handed people*. Do you play a particular musical instrument? Great! Try typing in *scholarships for saxophone players*. If you've decided on a particular college, type that in: *University of Michigan scholarships*, for example. Think about your interests, the academic subject you're majoring in, any minority group you're a member of, your geographical area, your religious affiliation, and any other aspect of your life that separates you from others. You can even try your hair color! Be creative and keep an open mind. Make sure you bookmark any potential scholarship websites you run across. If you're on a roll, you can come back later for a closer inspection to see if this is an opportunity you should pursue.

Cash Clue

Try typing in different combinations of words with quotation marks around various words combinations. In addition to the words scholarship and grant, think about qualities that set you apart such as ethnicity, race, and gender. Also use words that match up with your interests such as gymnastics and forensic science.

The Scholarship Databases

We talked earlier in this book about the different types of scholarship databases. These databases have scholarship information in them, and they'll try to match your personal information with those scholarships that their algorithms deem are matches.

Note that we're not totally confident that these systems work for all available scholarships. Our children, after all, won scholarships that weren't listed in these databases. So, we think they're a great place to start, but please, please, please don't limit yourself to them.

Also, some databases limit the kinds of scholarships in their databases. Some won't list any under $1,000 while others include scholarships as small as $50 (Rye, 2001).

Before you begin, it's important to go to your Internet browser and set up a bookmark folder. Actually, we used several bookmark folders. One was for scholarship search engines, and in that folder we bookmarked the websites we're listing in this chapter. But we also created bookmark folders for scholarships of particular interest, to be applied for later, and a folder for websites that have useful information for filling out applications, such as college websites.

It's tempting to stop your search for scholarship money with the 10 websites we're listing in this chapter. That sounds like a lot. In fact, that sounds like enough to find all of the scholarships in the world that you're eligible for. They are not, and we will show you other places to look. But for now, let's start with these.

Cash Clue

When you enter your information into these scholarship search engines, be as complete as possible so you get scholarship listings that are targeted to you as much as possible. Otherwise you can waste time going through scholarships that are more generic and more difficult to win.

FastWeb (http://www.fastweb.com)

This is a comprehensive scholarship search site online. Not only can you search for scholarships, but if your fill out your profile, FastWeb will send you e-mail alerts about new scholarships and deadlines. View scholarships in a list format, and delete the ones that don't apply to you. There also is information for high school educators and parents on this site.

FastWeb's site includes a variety of articles and discussion forums for students and parents, ranging from Social Media Do's and Don'ts for College Students, to 12 Tips on Paying for College in a Bad Economy.

FinAid! (http://www.finaid.org)

This is more than just a scholarship search engine. There also are cost estimators, information about loans and college savings, and tutorials to help you fill out forms. In addition, this site provides information about locating college loans.

College Board Scholarship Search (http://apps.collegeboard.com/cbsearch_ss/welcome.jsp)

You can view your SAT score here, as well as print a copy of your SAT essay. This search engine allows searching by location, cost, size, type of college, and more. There also is information about financial planning and finding the right school for you.

CollegeNET Scholarship Search (http://www.collegenet.com/elect/app/app)

You can search for scholarships by either keyword or profile. There also are forums on the site, which sometimes contain useful threads. Don't get sidetracked and spend too much time in the forums, no matter how much of an entertainment value they might have!

SuperCollege (http://www.supercollege.com)

SuperCollege has a scholarship search engine as well as a college search engine (for those of you who still haven't decided). There also is a large list of articles that can help you with your quest to fund your college education. Here is a sample list of articles:

✓ How to Choose the Right College
✓ How to Get Awesome Recommendations
✓ Effortlessly Recycle Your Admission Essays
✓ How to Avoid an Admission Essay Disaster

✓ Create a Killer College Application

✓ How to Find the Perfect Admission Essay Topic

Careers and Colleges (http://www.careersandcolleges.com)

As the name of this website implies, it focuses on careers and colleges. You can use a tool on the website to assess your career plans. Of course, the site wouldn't be complete without a scholarship search engine. The site also includes more than 4,000 college profiles.

Scholarships (http://www.scholarships.com)

Here is a website that delivers on its name, scholarships. It boasts having more than $19 billion of scholarships in its listings. You can search for local, state, and federal scholarships that are based on your academic achievements as well as your talents. It also has a tool to create scholarship application request letters.

Yahoo Scholarship Program Information (http://dir.yahoo.com/Education/ Financial_Aid/Scholarship_Programs)

This website doesn't have the depth as the others we've talked about, but it lists excellent scholarship opportunities. Here is a partial list of some of the scholarships you can find at this website:

✓ Montgomery GI Bill: Includes information and applications for the Montgomery GI Bill.

✓ United Negro College Fund (UNCF): Focuses on scholarships for historically black colleges and universities (HBCUS).

✓ International Education Financial Aid: Contains a searchable database of scholarships.

✓ Gates Millennium Scholars: Provides financial assistance to high-achieving minority students in financial need.

✓ Jackie Robinson Foundation: Helps students who aim to improve America for everyone.

Remember to record any passwords or usernames that you create as you navigate your way through these scholarship search engines and databases. We suggest you try to use the same ones whenever possible. This will save you a ton of time. Most of the time you can recover a password by having it reset or sent to your e-mail address after answering a hint question, but that's just another delay that can derail your train ride to scholarship glory.

Cash Clue

Before signing up for a scholarship search database, open a new e-mail account and use it just for your scholarship searches. That way, you won't miss out on something important because you thought it was spam.

OK, Now What?

It's going to take some time to work through your first scholarship application. You can save a bit of time by having a text file with your personal information (e.g., name, address, high school, GPA, and so on) written down. Then you can copy and paste from the text file into the application. But each application is slightly different, and you might as well work through the first one by taking your time and making sure that any information you enter into the application also goes into the text file. Your next application will take less than half the time of your first application, and the time will continue to decrease as your text file grows and you grow more proficient at the application process.

City	County	Region	State
Chamber of Commerce 123-4567	County Small Business Help 123-4567	Regional Commerce Organization 123-4567	University System 123-4567
Elks Lodge 123-4567	County Government 123-4567	Regional Group B 123-4567	State Representative 123-4567

Figure 6. Organizer to help find local, regional, and state scholarships.

Other Scholarship Sources

You've navigated your way around the Internet and have found plenty of scholarships to apply for. Now we're going to show you some other ways to find scholarship money. In a way, these methods offer better odds because they're local, thus reducing the pool of potential applicants.

Take a piece of paper, or a text file if you prefer working on a computer, and make four columns. You probably noticed by now that we value making notes and lists, and hopefully you've begun to see a method to the madness.

OK, back to the columns. Make a header for each column. Your four headers are city, county, region, and state. These will be locales for which you'll do some investigative work. The reason we add region to the list is because sometimes there are organizations that promote commerce and growth in an area that spans several counties. We live in such an area, the Piedmont Triad area in North Carolina, which encompasses Greensboro, High Point, and Winston Salem. There are scholarships available through these regional cooperatives.

In each column, you'll write down the phone number and contact names (if available) of organizations that might have scholarships available (see Figure 6). In the city column, get the telephone number of the chamber of commerce. Look through your telephone book to check if there are any VFW posts, Kiwanis Clubs, Elks lodges, Lions Clubs, and any other organization that has a chapter in your city. You usually can find these in a special section of the telephone book, usually under a heading such as "community." You also can check to see if these organizations have websites.

The game plan here is to call these numbers and ask if the organizations are sponsoring any scholarships. It's always a good idea to ask, too, if the person you're talking to knows of any other organization that is sponsoring scholarships for local students. You might stumble onto a little known scholarship that very few people apply for because it's not well-known or publicized.

Regional organizations might be trickier in finding contact information, but you can do it. Try using an online search engine to find the information. For example, we typed in Piedmont Triad into a search engine and added the word "commerce." We immediately found what we were looking for.

Your county should have a website, and there you'll find contact information. Write down the phone numbers in the appropriate column you've created. The same goes for your state.

This might sound like a lot of work when you can simply use the scholarship search engines and databases we listed earlier in this chapter. But the point is, you're doing extra legwork to try to find scholarships that aren't in the search engines. A lot of people aren't going to bother. This increases your odds of winning those scholarships because you put in the extra work to find them.

When you make each phone call, be sure to explain who you are and why you're calling. Don't overdo it, though. You don't want to give out your life story. But on the other hand, it's a good gesture to explain that you're heading off to college and are looking into local sources of scholarships and grants. Tell them your name to add a personal touch. And be sure to thank them, even if there are no sponsored scholarships. You can never tell when a moment of politeness will lead to a scholarship source.

Expand Your List

Take your list (print it if you've got it on your computer) to your high school counselor. Many times, high school counseling offices are very efficient at publishing information about scholarships, especially local ones. But it doesn't hurt to go in and ask about them. There might be new ones that have been created, or there could be ones that were missed in general announcements. Besides, it doesn't take much time to go in and ask, so just do it. Add this information to your list, in the appropriate column, of course.

Add more resources to your list by looking at the businesses listed on your city's chamber of commerce website. If it's a small business, chances are that it won't be sponsoring scholarships, and many of the larger businesses sponsor scholarships for children of employees, but we suggest you look at the list of businesses and try calling a few of the larger businesses that are listed.

Make sure you put the employers (past and present) of your parents on the list. These employers might offer scholarships, so get their phone numbers and add them to your list.

Local banks and credit unions are good places to put on your list, too. They tend to be involved with the communities in which they are established and sometimes sponsor scholarships to help maintain their image as businesses that are involved with their communities.

Be sure to ask your parents if they're members of any organization that might sponsor scholarships. Put them on your list.

OK, it's time to make those calls! Have pen and paper handy so that you can write down any information you're given.

Cash Clue

You probably know this, but we want to remind you that you can't believe everything you read on the Internet.

Information Overload

This is a chapter on finding information, and sometimes it can feel like information overload—especially if you have stacks of college brochures and application lying around.

We've suggested that you have folders on your computer so that you can keep your text files organized. Manila folders are a good idea, too. You can have one for the four-column list you just made, and in that folder you can put any follow-up information you get.

We suggest having a separate folder for each college that you're considering, a folder for each scholarship application that you complete (paper application, that is), and one for scholarship information and applications that you choose not to pursue.

Scholarship Spotlight

The Potato Industry Scholarship awards up to $5,000 for a graduate student who is pursuing studies in agribusiness (National Potato Council, 2009). For more details, visit http://www.nationalpotatocouncil.org.

7

Tools to Dig Up the Money

The D in GRAND SLAM

DEVELOP an action plan.

When you start applying for scholarships and searching for the right college for you, you're going to find yourself nearly overwhelmed at times with information. You might have a thousand things on your mind, things that need to get done. You might feel like throwing up your hands and say, "What do I do? What do I do?"

We're here to help you develop a plan, an action plan that will help you to achieve your scholarship money.

Scholarship Spotlight

The makers of Tylenol have a scholarship program that is currently in its 17th year. These scholarships go to students in the medical field and vary between $5,000 and $10,000. Scholarships are awarded based on leadership qualities and academic performance (McNeil Consumer Healthcare, 2009). For more details, visit http://www.tylenol.com/page.jhtml?id=tylenol/news/subptyschol.inc#.

Information

As you go through your search for scholarship money, you'll be running across all kinds of information. Some of the information will be given to you by the scholarship websites, and other kinds of information will be collected by you as input for the scholarship application. The more information you can save and store in a place you can easily find later, the quicker you'll be able to fill out other scholarship and admission applications.

Here are some of the types of information you'll want to save for later use.

✓ college admission requirements,
✓ tax and income numbers,
✓ scholarship and college links,
✓ your student profile, and
✓ essays.

Write down the information in a notebook dedicated to application information. You'll also run across items such as photocopies or print-outs of records, such as tax statements. Other types of information will be Internet addresses (URLs) that you can bookmark.

By organizing your information storage, you'll save hours and hours of time later. We were constantly fine-tuning our information storage system, and we marveled at how much time it saved us, especially when we considered that we used the system for five children. We've shared our system with coworkers, and they have thanked us countless times. Note that if you have any younger siblings or children who will be attending college in future years, you can pass along your information to them to aid in their scholarship search.

Cash Clue

Keep a master list of where you are saving your information, such as scholarship URLs, in a bookmark folder titled "Scholarships."

Journals

We've already suggested the use of journals in the self-evaluation process. Use another journal for scholarship application information. A spiral-bound notebook works well for this. You can, of course, create a text file on your computer. The advantage of a notebook is that it's portable. For example, you could bring it along when you tour a college campus. If you're talking to a high school counselor, you can write down tips the counselor gives you right there on the spot. You also could write down scholarship tips that local organizations might give you for winning their scholarships.

By keeping a separate journal for information you'll be using on scholarship applications, you'll be able to find it later. We've collected numerous spiral-bound notebooks, some with to-do lists, some with random notes and thoughts on the application process, and others with essay outlines. By dedicating one notebook for a specific type of information, we were able to find it quickly.

Benefits of Journals

Let's review a bit and see how journals helped our children during their search for scholarship money:

✓ The use of journals saved time. Our children didn't have to read the same information three or four times because they already knew where the answers were stored.

✓ The use of journals enabled them to keep track of the scholarship applications they had submitted. This saved them the frustration of not being sure if they had submitted an application or not.

✓ The use of journals helped give them a degree of confidence in their search for scholarships. This helped with essays and interviews.

Folders

Another important organizing tool is the use of manila folders. Why bring this up? After all, most of the scholarship applications will be completed online. The key word is *most*. You'll also be sending in paper applications and paper information. Whenever you do this, make a copy and put the copy in a manila folder. Label the folder so you can see what's inside at a glance.

You'll also be getting information via snail mail. Colleges will send you brochures, for example. There are some scholarship applications that will require letters of recommendation from people who know you. Sometimes the letters of recommendation are to be sealed so that you, the applicant, can't read the letter. This requirement is designed to help ensure the person who is writing the letter of recommendation gives an honest appraisal.

A manila folder is especially important for paper applications. Keep a separate folder for each application that requires a paper submission. For other scholarships that you've applied for online, print a copy of your application and put it in a folder that you label appropriately, such as Scholarship Applications Completed Online.

Case Study

We helped our neighbor's daughter apply for an Elks scholarship. This was a unique scholarship application process. The application was required to be hand-delivered to a local Elks lodge. There was a large package of materials she needed to accumulate that included the usual items—transcripts, letters of recommendation, and essays. The requirements were that these documents needed to be put into a 3-ring binder. Imagine the amount of time she would've needed if she hadn't been organized! And of course, because we had been telling our neighbor about the importance of being organized, the daughter kept good records. By staying organized during her scholarship application process, she was able to quickly accumulate the materials. As the deadline neared, she was able to three-hole punch her documents, put them in a binder, and drive to the local Elks lodge. Note that she called ahead to make sure someone was there to accept her application!

Filing Cabinet

Not everyone has a filing cabinet at home. Take a trip to a local resale store such as Goodwill. You usually can find an inexpensive used one there. Keep all of your manila folders in the appropriate file cabinet drawer. Another option is to use a portable plastic organizer or an accordion folder. Whichever you use, dedicate it to your scholarship folders. Keep nothing else in it. If you can't afford a file cabinet or don't have the room, keep your folders in one place, such as a bookshelf or a corner of a desk.

Cash Clue

The more disorganized your filing system is, the more time you'll waste hunting for materials and the more your search will lose focus. This can result in lost scholarship opportunities.

Spiral Notebooks

We've already talked about using spiral notebooks. If you haven't done so already, go out and purchase three or four spiral notebooks. They don't have to be the large ones with 200+ pages. Notebooks with 60 pages are fine. We've already suggested getting one for a journal, but you'll find the need for more as we go on with our hunt for free scholarship funding. You'll want one to practice essays, for example, and another for listing deadlines. Everyone has different needs, and you'll find yourself wanting a notebook at some point in your search. We have found that we wanted to have extra spiral notebooks on hand because we always had use for them.

Computer Folder System

You'll want a folder system on your computer, too, as well as manila folders for your paper copies. Some people save all their files to their computer desktop, but as with real desks, computer desktops can get messy and unorganized.

It's easy to create new folders on your computer. If you want to create a master folder on your desktop, that's fine. Another useful place on PC computers is the location My Documents or Documents. You also can use the Documents folder on your Macintosh computer. If you don't know how to create a folder, find someone to help you. It's an important skill you should know anyway, because you will need it.

Cash Clue

Some of the skills we talk about, such as creating a computer folder, are important to not only finding scholarships, but also being successful at college. You don't want to fully fund your college education with scholarship money only to get bad grades at school.

Where you create your master folder is up to you. But once you create it, immediately create subfolders within the master folder. Make sure you rename the folders so that you know what's in them at a glance. For example, you might name your master folder Scholarship Search. Then within that master folder, you could have the following subfolders.

- ✓ Essays
- ✓ FAFSA
- ✓ Scholarship Notes
- ✓ Scholarship Applications
- ✓ Completed Scholarships
- ✓ Pending Scholarships

Consider putting the year in the master folder. For example, you could name it 2010 Scholarship Search. This way, when you are reapplying for scholarships the following year, or applying for new scholarships, you can name it 2011 Scholarship Search and keep your applications organized.

In our computer folder system, we have a folder titled Scholarship Notes. You could create folders within the Scholarship Notes folder. For example, you could have a folder named Self-Evaluation or Career Thoughts for your journal entries. In any case, be sure to name your text file appropriately so that you know what's in it.

Cash Clue

We've suggested that you create a folder in your Internet browser where you can store the URLs of useful websites. You also can copy and paste the URLs into a text file and e-mail it to yourself so that you'll always have them handy and can find them when you're using a different computer.

Progress Charts

We also set up a bulletin board for our children. They used this board to chart their progress in the scholarship application process. They kept tally of the number of applications in progress, the number of applications submitted, and the number of scholarship application sessions they completed.

This enabled them to possess a degree of accomplishment as well as an idea of the progress they were making. Let's face it—there can be quite a lag time between all of the hours spent in applying for scholarships and the time that the scholarships are actually awarded. To combat this sense of not making progress, why not create your own progress chart? It doesn't have to be on a bulletin board. You can use a simple text file to accomplish the same thing. We suggest, however, that you print it out and put it someplace readily visible, such as the trusty refrigerator door.

Other Tips

We purchased a few books for our children to assist them in their scholarship searches. We found that writing in the margins of the books and highlighting certain passages was an excellent way to find information later.

Since the first time you picked up a crayon you've heard "Don't write in books!" We're changing that rule right now. Unless the book is school or library owned or you borrowed it from a friend, write in that book! Highlight important paragraphs and make notes to yourself in the margins. Not only will this save you time in your scholarship hunt, it's great training, because that's what you'll need to learn to do once you get in college. You can find many used books on college topics at half-price bookstores; these are really helpful for finding affordable resources that you can mark up.

You also can use sticky notes in the books. Maybe a book has a new scholarship you haven't heard about. A sticky note on the appropriate page will guide you later to the page so you can apply for it.

The Three-Item To-Do List

We talk about to-do lists a lot in this book. You can at times feel overwhelmed by these to-do lists. However, we found that having a quick to-do list is extremely helpful. There are things you need to do for scholarships, things you need to do for college admissions, things you need to do for self-evaluation, and many other things to do. We used a to-do list that was limited to three items. This was our *to-do asap* (as soon as possible) list. By keeping this list to three items, we didn't feel overwhelmed and we could stay focused on the things we need to do *today*.

Author Michelle C. Muratori (2007) noted that a "don't" list is important, too, and points out that one "don't" item should be to not wait until the last minute to write your to-do list.

Scholarship Spotlight

There is a scholarship called the Student-Athlete Milk Mustache of the Year (SAMMY). There are 25 annual winners of $7,500 for college. The winners also are inducted into the Milk House Hall of Fame (Body by Milk, 2009). For more details, visit http://www.bodybymilk.com/sammy_scholarship.php.

How to Get Going

The S in GRAND SLAM

SCHOLARSHIPS—find the ones you can win.

We've shown you some wonderful websites with scholarship databases and scholarship search engines. We've also shown you where to look locally for scholarship money. Now that you've found sources of scholarship money, it's time to implement strategies to find the ones you can win and get that scholarship money.

Scholarship Spotlight

Siemens Corporation has an annual competition called the Siemens Competition in Math, Science & Technology. This competition is based on submissions of science projects. The grand prize winner is awarded $100,000 (Siemens Corporation, 2009). For more details, visit http://www.siemens-foundation.org/en/competition.htm.

A Basic Questionnaire

OK, it's time for more self-analysis. We hope you've been writing in your journal, examining your motivations and thoughts about careers and colleges. When it's time to fill out scholarship applications, though, some of the questions can get more personal. Some scholarship applications will ask about your feelings on subjects such as global warming.

With this in mind, and based on our experience with scholarship applications, we've prepared a questionnaire for you. Create a text file and type in your answers. Give the questions some thought. It's good to write down your gut reactions, but scholarship judges look for answers that appear well thought out. We're not here to grade your responses, but remember that scholarship applications are graded, and the winners get the scholarship money. Below each question, we'll make a note about why these questions can be important on scholarship applications.

✓ *Have you visited a grandparent or other senior in a nursing home? Volunteered to read or sing carols at Christmas?* You might not think of yourself as someone who has done a lot of volunteer work, but perhaps you haven't considered that some of your activities can be looked upon as volunteer work. Scholarship judges tend to look favorably at applications that exhibit examples of students who have performed volunteer work.

✓ *Have you joined a parent in helping out at a soup kitchen, a shelter, or an animal rescue? Have you been in a class that participated in one of these activities?* Community service can be considered volunteer work, but it fits into a particular category that scholarship applications recognize. Because scholarships are monetary awards bequeathed to students, scholarship judges like to believe the winners of those scholarships are people who tend to give back to their communities.

✓ *Have you done extra activities at your place of worship, such as helping in the nursery, teaching younger children, or helping to serve dinners? How about selling raffle tickets or helping out at rummage or yard sales? Singing in a choir? Performing a play?* There are many activities performed in places of worship that scholarship judges will look favorably upon. Remember that one of the purposes of a scholarship application is to ask questions that will reveal the character of an applicant. You will want to fill out applications in such a way that shows you participate in activities that make your community stronger.

✓ *Is there an elderly or disabled neighbor that you help with yard work or other chores? Do you run errands for someone who is shut in?* Sometimes when you help a neighbor out, it's something that's done on the spur of the moment or perhaps at the bequest of a parent. But it should be considered volunteer work, and helping out the elderly or disabled exemplifies the best side of humanity. That's precisely the side of you that needs to be presented on scholarship applications.

✓ *Do you belong to any clubs or groups such as Scouts, YMCA, or a band?* Try to think about any group you're a member of or that you ever were a member of. These show your involvement in the community, and community involvement is something you want to list on your applications.

✓ *Do you enjoy any sports (besides the usual baseball, basketball, football, and soccer) including volleyball, table tennis, archery, hunting, or fishing? Are you a cheerleader?* People go to college to get educations and a degree, but college life isn't all study time. Scholarship judges also look at aspects of a student that exhibit a well-rounded nature. There's something to be said for the adage: "a healthy body leads to a healthy mind." Participation in sports (and we consider cheerleading an example of a sport) shows scholarship judges you're not one-sided.

✓ *Do you like to tinker inside the engine of a car or lawn-mower? How about inside a computer? Do you "have to know" what makes something work?* You might have a mechanical aptitude that will help you with some types of scholarships. Students going into engineering fields, for example, will benefit from being able to provide examples of this aptitude on applications.

✓ *Do you like to cook? Write your own computer games? Write stories or journals? Do you read a lot?* We hope that you've explored some of these types of questions in your journal as you examined your career aspirations. But it's time to look at these questions in a different light. When applying for scholarships, it will be beneficial to provide examples of your habits and activities that show you are who you say you are. If you are applying for a scholarship to major in English, it will be helpful to state you read an average of a book a week.

✓ *Do you play an instrument in the school band or at home or church? Are you in the marching band or concert band? Do you sing in the school choir?* Of course you'll want to list these kinds of activities if you're applying for a schol-arship in the field of music, but what if music isn't your major? It's good for a student to be focused on a major, but judges tend to favor well-rounded applicants.

✓ *Are you a member of any school clubs such as math, sci-ence, or English? How about history club, chess club, or the school paper? Did you work on the yearbook? Help organize homecoming or prom?* Think about your entire high school experience, going back to ninth grade. Any activities you performed outside the classroom will be good to put down on scholarship applications.

✓ *What are your three favorite classes through all of high school? What are your three favorite parts of each class?* Answering these questions will help give you food for thought on some of the scholarship application questions. Some applications might ask these very same questions! In any event, they will help you to answer essay questions. Remember that scholarship judges generally evaluate hundreds if not thousands of applications, and they can spot applications that have answers that took more thought and consideration. For example, if your three favorite classes are science, gym, and band, then you might list electrical experiments, conservation discussions, and chemistry labs as your three favorite parts of science. For gym, you might list playing baseball, jumping on a trampoline, and climbing a rope. You get the idea.

Cash Clue

When applying for scholarships, list *all* of your volunteer activities, including church activities. Ask your school counselor for places you can do volunteer work ASAP.

The Winning Scholarship Application

We've already mentioned some of the criteria that scholarship judges use to grade applications. They tend to look for students who are well rounded. Of course, they like students to have high grade point averages, but that's only one aspect they look at. Let's face it, if it was only a question of GPAs, then all you would to do on an application is list your personal information and your grades. The scholarship judges would simply plug the numbers into a program and the winners would pop out.

It's not that simple.

And we won't bother to list some of the examples of students who didn't have remarkable GPAs in high school and yet went on to achieve great success with their lives. Scholarship judges (and colleges) understand this, which is why they go through the trouble of having different questions on applications.

So be prepared to give examples of how you're a well-rounded individual. You want to list as many activities outside the classroom as you can. You want to be a volunteer who has participated in community projects. You want to have the right frame of mind—eager and determined to learn and achieve. Your answers to questions should appear well thought out. Your essays should be polished and error free.

Some scholarships require students to have a particularly high interest in a subject or field of study. Some experts note that scholarship administrators understand that most applicants are young and have interests that can change. They suggest you apply for these scholarships even if your interest is only mild (Kaplan, 2002).

The First Thing to Look At

It might sound simple, but it's something we've wasted time on. The first thing to look at on a scholarship listing is eligibility. We know, actually it's the second thing, with the amount of the scholarship typically being the first. We understand. Been there, done that. But you want to make sure you meet the eligibility requirements before reading too much about the scholarship.

And there's a bonus, actually, to developing the habit of looking at eligibility requirements first.

As is the case with our son Scott, we discovered a scholarship that had as it main eligibility requirement that the applicant is the child of a retired military service member. Bingo. Not only was Scott eligible for this scholarship (as were our other children), but this disqualified many other high school students, reducing the pool of potential applicants.

The Best Way to Start

The best way to start is to apply for a scholarship. Go to the scholarship search websites we list in this book, find an appropriate scholarship, and then apply for it. As you're filling out the application form, remember to keep a text file copy of all of the information you enter.

Don't be discouraged at the amount of time you'll need to fill out your first application. It actually might take you several days, depending on how much information you have on hand. For example, the application might ask for your high school grade point average. If you don't have that number handy, you'll have to contact your high school registrar and go through the process of obtaining it.

While you're getting your grade point average, ask for a copy of your high school transcript, if you haven't already. At some point during the scholarship application process, you'll need a copy of your high school transcript.

Cash Clue

Scan a copy of your high school transcript into a computer file. You don't need a high resolution copy. Some applications can be completed online if you can send e-mail attachments that contain pictures of your high school transcript. If your file size is too large, you might be limited in what you can apply for. Find someone to help if you're unsure how to scan a transcript into a computer file.

We found that, for our children, the first couple of scholarship applications took several evenings to complete. But by the time we got to the third application, we were cutting the time by half. And after a few more applications, our children could complete an application in an hour or two. Sometimes the main delay was the requirement for an essay. Read the application instructions carefully to see if the essay must be original. If not, you can use your essays over and over.

It doesn't hurt, though, to freshen up your essays from time to time. As with any piece of writing, there is always room for improvement. And of course, you'll run into essay topics that you haven't covered yet with a previous essay. These will require you to write a new one. We cover essay writing extensively in another chapter in this book. We believe essays are extremely important in winning scholarship money, so don't take the essay lightly!

What We've Seen

From our experience, the process of filling out scholarship applications needs to be done with a particular frame of mind. Remember that these applications are judged in relation to hundreds or thousands of other applications. What's going to set yours apart from the others? What is going to be the deciding factor in your application winning the scholarship money?

Of course the answer varies from scholarship to scholarship. But there are common threads to winning applications. First, they are mistake-free. All of the questions have been answered, and all of the requested information has been supplied. We believe if these three things are accomplished, you'll already be ahead of many other applications.

Students who are confident in their abilities also write applications that win scholarships. You might not have the highest grade point average in your high school, but you should feel confident that you can be successful in college, that you can handle the increased academic workload, and that you'll be a net positive for the college you attend because you intend to participate in student activities and contribute to the community.

If you have doubts about any of the above, we suggest you get out your journal and write some personal passages about why you should feel this way. Because when sponsors of scholarships hand out the money, they want to feel comfortable that the money will be used by students who will be successful. Otherwise, why give out the scholarship in the first place?

So remember that having a positive attitude will help you to fill out a winning scholarship application.

Cash Clue

If you find yourself near the end of the evening and you're filling out an application, but you're tired and are rushing, perhaps almost blindly, to complete the application just to get it out of the way, stop for the night. Finish the application the following day. When you're tired, you're more prone to make mistakes and your answers will tend to sound uninspired.

Tricky Application Questions

We have found that most scholarship application questions are straightforward. They might ask for your opinion on this subject or that topic. But once in a while you'll find a question that appears tricky.

These questions usually aren't meant to be confusing, but because the people who put these applications together are human, the grammar and sentence structure can sometimes be less than crystal clear. For example, we've run across questions that have three of four preface sentences followed by a question that is hypothetical but written as though it were real.

If you come across a question that appears confusing, you have a couple of options, and we've used both. Copy and paste the question into a text document. Make each sentence in the question into its own paragraph. Then you can read each sentence and break down its meaning individually.

Or you can try reading the question slowly and aloud to another person, perhaps a parent or friend. Sometimes hearing the question and talking about it can make its meaning clearer.

If you're still confused, visit the website from which you

obtained the application. See if there are any instructions that clarify the question. Some of these websites also have user forums. You could check for posts there and see if any address your questions. If not, you could try posting a comment yourself and ask if anyone has insight. Scholarship websites often list an e-mail address for anyone who has questions, so you could try that, also. Remember, we believe your scholarship application answers need to convey a tone of surety and confidence, which is difficult to achieve if you have a degree of uncertainty about a question. It's better to wait for explanations so that you will feel sure about what the question is asking.

Scholarship Spotlight

Llama lovers in Michigan can try to win the Llamafest Annual Scholarship, which is sponsored by the Michigan Llama Association. This scholarship is awarded to a student who will attend the College of Veterinary Medicine at Michigan State University (Michigan Llama Association, 2009). For more details, visit http://www.michiganllama.org/about.html.

9

Write a Winning Essay

The L in GRAND SLAM

LEARN how to write good essays. There are a lot of people who will be applying for scholarships who have good grades, financial need, and a host of extracurricular activities. By learning how to write an essay that wows the judges, you'll be a step ahead of most other applicants.

Scholarship Spotlight

The Glen Miller Birthplace Foundation offers scholarships for instrumentalists and vocalists. Scholarships are awarded to high school seniors and college freshmen. Applicants must submit a high-quality audio CD or tape. Finalists perform live auditions (The Glen Miller Birthplace Foundation, 2009). For more details, visit http://www.glennmiller.org/scholarships.html.

The Essay That Blew Us Away

We want to give you some advice for writing essays that will win scholarships for you. Understand that many essay questions are quite broad, and they leave you with a lot of leeway. The best essays are revealing and specific in nature. Some authors suggest essays should be fun to read (Simpson & Spencer, 2009). We suggest they should, at a bare minimum, be engaging.

We've read a lot of our children's essays. We've provided input, did some grammar and spelling checks, and generally told them which sections were the strongest and which seemed weaker. Of course we backed up our opinions with why we felt that way.

But when our son Scott wrote an essay about his work as a volunteer at a summer camp, it blew us away. Part of the reason was because it was so personal in nature. It revealed something about him that we didn't know. And it also showed how he was building character right before our eyes!

The essay described how he was volunteering to be a mentor at a summer day camp for the disadvantaged. Scott really isn't the type of person to be the first to volunteer for anything, and as he explained in his essay, he was actually doing it to pad his resume for college.

But, the essay continued, he had a change of heart by the second day. It's one thing to understand how kids will be appreciative of the opportunity to be at summer camp, but it's another thing to see it in their eyes. And this is what Scott wrote about. He had known intellectually about how the act of giving can be beneficial for those who give, but he'd never felt it before. It was an experience that expanded his horizons and he described it beautifully.

This was the essay that helped get him into the North Carolina School of Science and Math, guaranteeing him a scholarship to any college in North Carolina.

Two Essay Types

Most scholarship applications allow you to take all of the time in the world (at least until the application deadline) to write, rewrite, and otherwise hone your essay. In some situations, however (e.g., the PSAT's National Merit Scholarship Qualifying Test), the essays must be completed within a set amount of time.

We'll talk mostly about the first type. Once you have some practice in writing essays and have the opportunity to polish them and make them stronger, you'll learn techniques that will apply to the timed essays.

Where Do I Start?

You've got a blank sheet of paper (or computer monitor) and an essay question. Getting started often is the most difficult part of an essay for many people. There's an endless number of ways in which to put those first few sentences down. Once they're written, however, the ensuing sentences will flow from those that preceded them.

If the essay is forming rapidly in your mind and you're itching to start, by all means go ahead! At any point when writing, if you feel the creative juices flowing and the sentences come spilling out from your fingertips, go, go, go! This will almost always be representative of your best work. The reason? It's because you're writing with passion, and the passion will show in the writing, and the scholarship judges will recognize that passion and give good grades accordingly.

We'll get to that in a minute, but first we're talking about people who're having a difficult time getting started.

Remember how to do those old-fashioned outlines with Roman numerals? Do it!

It's a great way to get the spine of an essay constructed. The flow of logic in an essay that has been outlined will be more apparent. For each main point raised in the outline, have supporting arguments and acknowledgements of other points of view. Remember that with any essay, the first and last paragraphs will cover the main thesis or topic of the essay, with the last paragraph wrapping up your argument.

So get started by writing an outline. And start your outline by writing a thesis sentence. For example, Scott's thesis sentence could be: "People from my parents to my teachers have always told me that volunteer work is a very satisfying and rewarding experience, but it wasn't until I volunteered at summer camp that I understood what they meant."

Some Typical Essay Questions

We've seen some fairly standard essay questions over the years. We've compiled our versions of these questions for you. It's a good idea to write an essay about each and every one of these questions, even if you don't feel like it would be one of your strongest essay topics. Why? If you apply for a scholarship that requires an interview, these same questions often will reappear during the interview. Won't it be great if you're in an interview and one of these questions is asked, and you've already written an entire essay on the subject? We believe it will work to your benefit.

- ✓ What do you want to do or accomplish with your life? Why do you feel that way?
- ✓ Is there anyone who has had a special impact on your life? Who was it? What was the impact? Has this made you a better person?
- ✓ Whom do you admire? Why? (Note: You had better think of someone worthy of admiration! Parents are a good, safe choice, but a particular teacher is even better. Sometimes you can let it slip in that it's a tie between two people.)
- ✓ What is your greatest achievement in life? Why do you feel it's your greatest achievement?
- ✓ What have you done to help people in general?

✓ If you were President, what would be your first priority? (In general, be prepared to talk about climate change, the economy, world conflicts, energy consumption, and global hunger.)

✓ What do you think is the world's most urgent problem?

Cash Clue

Read. Read books, magazines, newspapers. Read online and paper copies. As every writer knows, reading improves one's writing skills.

Some Questions

Ask yourself questions if you're not sure where to start with your essay. Here are some questions to ask yourself to help you along.

✓ What am I trying to say?

✓ What could I say that is different because of my unique perspective?

✓ What's the first thing that comes into my mind when I read this essay question?

✓ What would I need to find out in order to have a more informed opinion on this?

As you get better accustomed to asking yourself questions, you'll narrow in on the aspects of the essay question that are giving you difficulties in coming up with a response.

Overused Essay Topics

Some essay topics have been overused and are not interesting anyway, except perhaps to the writer. Essay graders will look unfavorably at essays written about a student's luxury tour, a listing of sights seen, or a travel wish list (Wissner-Gross, 2006).

Free Writing

We mentioned that if your fingers are taking off and the words are flowing, keep going. One of the drills we have our children practice is something called "free writing." The trick here is to write fast and not worry about grammar, spelling, or even what you're saying. Just . . . keep . . . writing. It's a method for tapping into the subconscious, or at least into a deeper layer of the brain, a place where we place fewer restrictions on ourselves.

We suggest trying this two or three times. You might be surprised at the result. In any event, it will help you with the creative side of your essays.

After the Outline

Write the first draft. The key word in that sentence is "first." A lot of people put so much pressure on themselves to come up with perfect prose the first time out that they end up constricting their writing. There's no flow. True, these essays may be mistake free, but you can be assured that there are plenty of essay responses to scholarship questions that are mistake free. Your job is to come up with an essay that's good enough to win a scholarship, and that's going to require going beyond mistake free.

So free yourself up to make some mistakes in the first draft. Focus on getting your main ideas down. Follow your outline if you have one, but if you find yourself writing intently about a topic and it takes you in a new direction, go there. You can always edit later. We're of the mind that it's easier to cut words out of an essay than to add them, so by all means let those words flow.

The Second Draft and Critiques

With our children, we went ahead with our critiques on their first drafts. We would rather see all of the glaring grammar errors and out-of-place sentences while at the same time trying to glean what the best parts of the essays were.

However, we suggest going through the first draft and cleaning it up a little before sending it out for critique. Misspelled words, misplaced commas, and dangling modifiers can be distracting. The people who are critiquing the essay will spend valuable time correcting mistakes that would have been corrected anyway. So clean up the essay for a second draft, then send it to friends and family, and perhaps most importantly, an English teacher, for some feedback.

When you get the feedback, keep an open mind. If more than one person says the same thing about it, then it's probably a valid point. Sometimes you'll get opinions that are in opposition with each other. Seek out a third party and discuss it. Remember, you're trying to write an excellent essay that will garner the interest of scholarship judges, so getting input from a variety of people is in your best interest.

Later and Final Drafts

Take the comments from the people who have read your essay and revise the essay. Send it out for another review. Continue this process until the essay is as good as you think it can be. There will come a point when you know you've done all you can. That's the point at which you submit your essay.

The Scholarship Journal

As you proceed through the scholarship application process, it's great to carry around a small notebook with you. Whenever a thought strikes you that could be useful in an essay, write it in your notebook. Then, once a week, go through your notebook and transfer these thoughts to a scholarship journal.

The scholarship journal is where you develop winning scholarship ideas. Remember, the best essays come from your heart. Believe us, judges can tell if an essay is contrived or not. You want to write essays that are completely original. Because most normal human beings don't have a clue as to when those brilliantly original thoughts will strike, we need to have notebooks handy so we can write them down.

The 10-Essay Challenge

If you believe us when we say that writing outstanding essays could be the skill that lifts you above others in the scholarship awarding process, then doesn't it make sense to try to become quite proficient at it?

We challenged our children to write 10 essays. They didn't have to show them to us, and they didn't have to go beyond the first draft. But we wanted them to get in the habit of organizing their thoughts into essay form, and we did have another reason that we failed to mention. This is excellent practice for writing essays that are timed, such as the essay questions on SAT exams.

It was a kind of game we played, and we changed the rules after they were done writing their essays. Although we had told them they didn't have to show them to us, we asked to see the essays. They still had the option to keep them private, but we told them we could help improve their essay-writing skills. Actually, we found out that they didn't finish 10 essays. They each wrote between three and five, but what the heck, if we had asked them to write five, they would've written two. We suspect high school students reading this will know where we're coming from. In any event, we were able to look over their essays and point out their strengths. Lynn's prose tended to shine when she wrote about young children and helping them learn and grow. Scott's essays excelled when he wrote about personal experiences. You get the idea. This helped them improve their ability to select essay topics, which is important because many scholarship applications give you a choice of essay topics. If you know what your strengths are, you'll be better prepared to write a winning essay!

Six Rules for Timed Essays

When you're taking the PSAT or SAT, you have a specific amount of time in which to complete your essay. Although most scholarship applications won't have this time restriction, you could find yourself in that position.

With that in mind, we'll give you our six rules to help you write a shining essay within the time limit. They might help you to write essays that are not time-constrained, so we encourage you to read on even if you've already taken the PSAT or SAT!

Rule #1: Sketch Out Preliminary Ideas

You'll have some initial thoughts regarding your essay question. Write them down. Then write down some "maybe good" ideas. Once you've got a lot of ideas written down, you have a lot to work with. Isn't that better than looking at a blank piece of paper?

Rule #2: Pick Out Your Good Ideas and Arrange Them

For the purpose of essay writing, good ideas are ones you feel strongly about and for which you can think of supporting arguments. An idea might be a great idea, but if there's no supporting argument, you won't convince the essay graders.

Rule #3: Write Out a Quick Outline of Your Ideas

You should always start and end with the strongest ideas, with the most supported one coming at the end. The reason for this is that is leaves a good impression with the grader right before giving out a grade. Try to have all of the ideas be connected to each other with some line of thought or reasoning.

Rule #4: Write Your Essay

Go slowly but deliberately. It's better to have an excellent short essay than a good long one. Keep your grammar and spelling as clean as you can, although in general they don't count as much as the flow of your arguments.

Rule #5: Write a Strong Conclusion

After making your last point or argument, summarize your essay by repeating your main points and how they support your thesis sentence.

Rule #6: Do a Final Read-Through

Read through your essay to check for any last-minute errors you might've made. This is your last chance to make corrections and make a positive impression on the grader.

A Few Final Words on Essays

Write your essays on topics you care about whenever possible Judges will know that you care about the topic. Your passion will shine through.

We're going to drift back to the outline. It's helpful sometimes to think about how essays are constructed, and we suggest reading opinion pieces in the newspaper to get examples. Once you become accustomed to thinking about a topic in outline form, you're on your way to writing excellent essays!

Whether you're ending an essay or a chapter in a book (like we are now), it's good to keep on topic, and we're going to suggest that writing a strong conclusion to an essay is vital to impacting the judges. The final sentence in the essay should be succinct.

Like the sentence preceding this one.

Scholarship Spotlight

The Klingon Language Institute offers a scholarship to promote the study of language. Knowledge of the Klingon language is not required, although scholarship applicants are encouraged to be creative (Klingon Language Institute, 2009). For more details, visit http://www.kli.org/scholarship.

10

Scholarship Application Sessions

The Second A in GRAND SLAM

APPLY for scholarships and for admission into the college that's right for you. Nearly all of our children's scholarship applications were submitted during a scheduled scholarship application session. By scheduling weekly sessions, they were able to get traction on the process. We've passed along this regimen of weekly scholarship sessions to friends and neighbors, and it has worked for their children, too.

We've talked about how to find the best fit/match between you and a college, and now's the time to apply for admission if you haven't already. We've given you our GRAND SLAM method for winning college scholarships (except the **M**, *maintain your advantage by following up*, which we discuss in a later chapter), and now we'll tell you about how our children tailored this strategy for their own efforts. Everyone has a different way of doing things, so we certainly don't want to present these steps in a form that is not pliable. Rather, we prefer you tinker with the strategy and adapt it to your needs.

Cash Clue

You must have the attitude that no scholarship is too small. OK, maybe $3.50 is too small, but a $250 scholarship is something to apply for! You don't have to shoot for the several thousand-dollar scholarship every time. Small ones add up, especially if you get 10 of them! We speak from experience here, as a few of our (unnamed) children have scoffed initially at the smaller scholarships. But after we pointed out that there would be few applicants for these smaller scholarships, their interest ramped up.

A Time and Place

We happen to understand that we are creatures of habit. Not everyone likes to be so regimented. We do. We're not averse to changing our habit, and we enjoy spur of the moment decisions, but by and large we like to know how each hour of the day ahead will be spent. Usually, it's the same as some previous day because we've developed so many firm habits. So we're going to suggest that you set aside a time and a place for your scholarship application sessions. It could be right after dinner in the den. If you'll be using a desktop computer for your session, the place will be wherever your computer is located. But if you have a laptop computer, you'll be able to choose a place. Pick someplace quiet, a place where you'll have minimal distractions and interruptions.

Set aside 2 hours for each of your scholarship sessions if possible. We've found that 90 minutes is generally a minimum for having a productive session. If your session runs shorter than this, you won't be making efficient use of the time. This is because it generally takes 10 to 15 minutes to get cranked up; that is, to find your bookmarks and journals and notes, or get yourself to where you were at the end of your last scholarship session.

Cash Clue

Remember that the people who evaluate scholarship applications can tell who has put a lot of work into their applications, so we suggest you double check all of your submissions and give them a final coat of polish.

Apply for Scholarships, Take Notes

Use your scholarship sessions to apply for scholarships. If you come across a roadblock, some piece of information or a form that you need to complete the application, write down what you need and move on. Be sure to take notes. A scholarship journal is useful at this point, so you can write down the name of the scholarship and the date on which you applied. Bookmark websites that have the scholarships you're applying for.

We've given you hints and tips throughout this book on winning scholarships. These scholarship application sessions are when you bring all of these techniques and strategies to bear.

Also, if you happen to go through an entire scholarship session without actually completing an application, don't despair. Remember that the search for scholarship funding, if compared to a race, is more of a marathon than a sprint. The student who maintains a steady pace and keeps going for the long haul will be the student who ends up winning the scholarships. The student who puts in a few long nights and becomes quickly exhausted might win a scholarship or two, but there will be many missed scholarship opportunities.

Cash Clue

Watch out for scams! Although there are legitimate services that cost money to aid in scholarship searches, there are many that will take your money and do no more than you can easily do yourself online.

Scholarship Applications

Some hints for completing scholarship applications: Don't miss those deadlines! You can set up e-mail reminders with Microsoft Outlook, iCal, or other computer applications. Sticky notes work as well. Go over your applications a second time after you've completed them. We've been guilty of filing incomplete applications. After all, we can get in a hurry just like anyone else. So when you're finished, take a step back and go get a drink or snack. Take a deep breath and look over each question on the application to ensure you've filled everything out. Double check the length of your essay. Get as close to the word count that the essay question asks for without going over. You can copy and paste your essay into a word processing application (many of which will count the words for you). If you don't know how to get a word count, find someone who does. You'll need to know when you get to college (with your full funding!).

Scholarship Spotlight

The Alzheimer's Foundation of America has a scholarship program called AFA Teens for Alzheimer's Awareness College Scholarship. This is a $5,000 scholarship awarded to a student based on an application that includes a written autobiography and an essay about Alzheimer's disease (Alzheimer's Foundation of America, 2009). For more details, visit http://afateens.org/about_new.html.

Although it's important not to miss deadlines, some experts believe that applications should be sent close to the deadlines and not too early. Early filers might find their applications looked over with a fine-tooth comb (Chany & Martz, 2006).

Cash Clue

For scholarships that require many different submission materials, keep a checklist in that scholarship's folder for an easy way to keep track of your progress.

Catching Up

If you miss a scholarship session, you can catch up by scheduling another session the next day. The important thing is to set aside a specific number of hours per week that you feel are a minimum. Of course, if you can put in more hours, great! But take the weekend, for example, and work on scholarship applications if you miss one of your sessions. The hours and applications will eventually add up, winning scholarship money for you.

Do These!

We do think you should apply for as many scholarships as possible. Obviously there are some scholarship opportunities that you should definitely apply for, especially when compared to other opportunities. For example, if you find a scholarship that's available to residents of the county in which you live, it's a scholarship that should be at the top of your list. Regardless of the population of your county, the pool of applicants will be significantly smaller than the pool for a scholarship that is open nationwide. You thereby increase your chances of winning.

Pay attention to the latest government programs, too, which can be initiated quickly in response to economic conditions. For example, there are government agencies rushing to provide scholarship and grant money to laid-off workers during the current economic downturn (Clark, 2009).

Cash Clue

Many people pay consultants big bucks to get their teen into the "right" college, only to find out months later that their son isn't happy and doesn't fit in. Other people have lost good money by paying for "guaranteed" results, only to find out it was a flash in the pan scam to get their hard-earned cash. If you decide to hire someone, make sure you get references from consultants, contact the references, and verify you know what you're getting.

Letters of Recommendation

During your scholarship application session, you'll come across an application that requires a letter of recommendation (or several). If you don't have one yet, this can be a roadblock. Make sure to put a sticky note that lists your missing requirement on the refrigerator.

Letters of recommendation can sometimes be supplied as a form that a teacher or school administrator needs to fill out on behalf of the student. More often, however, letters of recommendation are from people who know you and are willing to state your achievements and abilities and that they feel you would be a good candidate for the scholarship.

Who do you ask? Usually the application will specify that it not be a relation, so that leaves out your parents. Sometimes they will specify that it come from a teacher; sometimes they leave it up to you. Good prospects to ask for letters are teachers, school officials such as principals and counselors, instructors of extracurricular activities such as coaches and private music teachers, Scout leaders, ministers, employers, and local business persons with whom you're familiar. Don't forget to consider friends of your parents and family; Mom's coworker might be the perfect person.

Cash Clue

Different colleges have different deadlines for admission applications, FAFSA submissions, and other materials. Be sure to check with the colleges you're applying to for their specific deadlines.

Important Considerations

The person you ask should be able to write fairly well. You don't want a letter of recommendation that contains numerous spelling and grammatical errors. The writer should be able to translate thoughts into words, so the letter makes sense and impresses the reader. Make sure he or she is able to write the letter in a timely manner. Some people are natural-born procrastinators; if someone keeps putting you off, you need to ask another person.

Once you've come up with a list of people who you feel will be good candidates to recommend you, read the application requirements again and make a simple outline for the writer to follow so he or she doesn't forget to answer a specific point. For instance, an application might ask how you've contributed to your community, examples of your achievements, and what your work habits are like. A short list of bulleted points is great for this.

Below your bullets of items required, make a list of your accomplishments so your letter writer can refer to them. The person might not be aware of everything you've done, or may draw a blank when he or she sits down to write. Use a different type of bulleting so it's easy to distinguish.

Attach an example of an essay you've written for the scholarship you're applying for or one that you've written that tells about your plans and goals. This will help your recommendation writer to get a better feel for your objectives.

Give the person as much time as possible when you're asking

for a letter of recommendation. Two weeks is perfect. You can call him at the end of the first week with a reminder of your deadline. If the writer seems to falter, ask him if another scholarship deadline would work better. This will give your recommender a gracious out if he can't find the time to write a good letter.

Don't take for granted that someone you know well and respect will give you a good recommendation! You'll see what we mean in the following case study. We're leaving the names out on this one. You'll see why when you read it.

Cash Clue

Depending on your work habits, you might want to work on applications for short periods of time. If you spend 15 minutes on an application and start feeling impatient, save your files and take a break.

Case Study

One of our kids needed a letter of recommendation for a very prestigious award; we're talking upwards of $50,000 over 4 years. They confidently asked their favorite teacher, one they'd had classes with for all 4 years of high school (and a straight 4.0 GPA to boot). After receiving the letter in a sealed envelope as required by the grant application guidelines they noticed they could see through the envelope that the teacher had forgotten to sign the form: an automatic disqualification. After tossing the envelope in the trash, curiosity got the better of the teen and they fished it out to read what their mentor had written.

Imagine the shock when they found that the same teacher who praised them endlessly in person had given them a bad letter of recommendation and said they didn't feel this student was a wise choice for the application board to award the grant to!

Crushed but wiser, the student asked another person to give them a letter of recommendation; but only if they felt they could honestly write a good one.

Scholarship Spotlight

The American Society for Enology and Viticulture offers scholarships to students who major in studies that emphasize the science of the wine and grape industry. The scholarship amounts vary from year to year (American Society for Enology and Viticulture, 2009). For more details, visit http://asev.org/scholarship-program.

The Interview

11

Why This Chapter?

WHEN we began writing this book, we had our strategy for giving a terrific interview in another chapter. One reason for this was because an interview, time-wise, is such a very small part of the overall scholarship application process.

But then we realized time wasn't the most significant factor in an interview—it's the importance of the interview that matters. The interview usually is the final step for judging applicants that decides which ones will get the scholarships and which ones won't.

Scholarship Spotlight

The American Planning Association lists numerous scholarships and fellowships designed to help students achieve their educational goals. In addition to scholarships and fellowships from the American Planning Association, it lists scholarships from other organizations. It also sponsors an essay writing contest (American Planning Association, 2009). For more details, visit http://planning.org/scholarships/index.htm.

Interview Tips

We've already touched on interviews as part of the scholarship application process. Generally, if you've made it to an interview, you've already made it past part of the screening process. Conducting interviews is a time-intensive prospect for scholarship sponsors, so they don't want to give interviews to everyone who applies. Rather, they weed out many applicants on the paper part of the application. If you've made it to an interview, congratulations. You're already a cut above most of the other applicants.

You'll want to prepare for the interview. Study questions that might be asked. These often are the same questions that we've listed in the chapter about writing essays. Now, however, you'll have to give the answers off the top of your head. As long as you're familiar with the subjects, you'll do OK. After all, the questions will be about how you feel about certain topics and your college and career plans. By the time you've applied for numerous scholarships, and you've been writing in your journal all along, you'll have a degree of confidence that will be missing in some of the other interviewees.

Dress appropriately, meaning that you should consider dressing as though you were going in for a job interview. Dress conservatively. A suit and tie works for males, and an appropriate dress or business-style suit should be worn by females. A moderate amount of jewelry is OK, but don't overdo it. Don't forget the shoes—a nice-looking dress worn with flip-flops may be a turnoff to interviewers (and they're certainly not business attire!).

Be on time for your interview. This means that you should plan on arriving early. If you're late, you can forget about getting the scholarship. Why would a judge pick someone who can't be on time for something so important?

When you're called in for your interview, walk confidently into the room and greet the judges. Remember they've interviewed many applicants, so you'll stand out in their minds if you make a conscious effort to make a personal connection with them. Be professional, though, and not chummy.

Look the interviewers in the eyes when you respond. Keep your hands relaxed, on your lap or knees. Don't clench your hands or fidget.

Your answers should fully address the question. We know this is a judgment call, but you don't want your answers to be too long or too short. Try to find a happy medium. You can sometimes tell by the interviewers' hands or faces if you're talking too long about a particular subject, because they will start to get fidgety and impatient.

After the interview is over, be sure to thank the interviewers for their time, then leave the room.

Cash Clue

Practice being interviewed "under the lights." That is, find someone with a video camera that has a light function. The light will help dramatize the intensity of the interview process. Record your interview, having a friend or family member ask questions that are written out on 3" x 5" index cards. After the interview is over, watch the recording and ask family members for ways to improve your performance. By practicing interviews, you can improve to the point where you feel comfortable you'll do well, and that's a very good feeling indeed!

Case in Point

When our daughter Lynn was going in for an interview, she asked if we could drive her to the location. It was in Chapel Hill, NC, which was a drive of about 2 hours from our home. During the drive, we were able to talk to her about the country's social issues and ask her questions about what she wanted to do with her life. We gave her some pointers about how to clarify some of her answers or to make them more poignant.

Lynn was so pleased when she won her scholarship, and she attributed her success in the interview to the drive to Chapel Hill. It relaxed her, she claimed, and made her feel comfortable in giving her answers.

When you go in for your interview, it might be a good idea to bring along some family members for moral support, although if any of your family members are antagonistic toward you (which siblings can sometimes be), pick a couple of friends to tag along instead.

After the interview was over, Lynn explained to us about something she did that she later claimed won her the scholarship. Keep this in mind! When the interview was over, the interviewers asked if she had any questions. From the material we'd been given that discussed the interview process, we all knew that the interviewers were intimately involved in educational administration. So when they asked if Lynn had any questions, she was genuinely curious and asked how they felt about the No Child Left Behind Act. They expressed their opinions and then complimented Lynn on having such an excellent question. We realized later they probably asked themselves the very same question from time to time.

Cash Clue

Just like with essays, when you can inject passion into an answer, it's a good thing. You certainly don't want to come across as giving answers by rote. Anyone can memorize an answer, but not everyone can be passionate about a subject, and unless you're applying for scholarships in the acting profession, your fellow interviewees might not be able to give impassioned answers.

Interview Questions

In our chapter on writing essays, we listed our compilation of typical essay questions. If you take our suggestion, you'll write essays about the questions. Even if you don't come across scholarships that have these specific questions in the applications, you'll gain practice in essay writing, and you'll be better prepared if the question comes up during an interview. Many of these same questions will be asked during interviews, and because they're so important, we'll list them again. As you read through them, try answering them aloud, off the top of your head. No pressure—the answer is between you and yourself. But we believe by doing this, you'll be training your subconscious to come up with good answers.

- ✓ What do you want to do or accomplish with your life? Why do you feel that way?
- ✓ Is there anyone who has had a special impact on your life? Who was it? What was the impact? Has this made you a better person?
- ✓ Whom do you admire? Why? (Note: You had better think of someone worthy of admiration! Parents are a good, safe choice, but a particular teacher is even better. Sometimes you can let it slip that it's a tie between two people.)
- ✓ What is your greatest achievement in life? Why do you feel it's your greatest achievement?
- ✓ What have you done to help people in general?
- ✓ If you were President, what would be your first priority? (In general, be prepared to talk about climate change, the economy, world conflicts, energy consumption, and global hunger.)
- ✓ What do you think is the world's most urgent problem?

If you have an interview approaching, go back and read through your essays. They will often help you gain a degree of confidence for the interview, and you'll be able to speak at length on a number of topics.

Our Interview Rules

We've boiled down our interview advice into six strategies. Adhere to them, and you'll have a great interview, improving your chances of winning that scholarship.

Strategy #1: Know How to Stay Relaxed

At least, stay as relaxed as possible. Some people say that a little bit of tension is all right. It keeps you on your toes. We agree with that. But note also our rule is not "Stay Relaxed." That's easy to say. What's harder is knowing what helps you to relax. Is it slow, controlled breathing? Does reading help you relax? How about listening to you MP3 player? (If it's the last one, make sure it's turned off and hidden from view before the interview.)

Strategy #2: Make Eye Contact

If you don't have good eye contact with the interviewer, you're not going to be graded well. People who look away while they speak are thought of as fabricating the answers or at least stretching the truth. Don't stare, and do look away occasionally, but make sure you have good eye contact with the person conducting the interview.

Strategy #3: Have a Good Appearance

Dress well, like you're going in for a job interview, and conservatively. No jeans or sandals! Don't overdo it with cologne, perfume, or make-up. That can't help you, and it sure can hurt. If you need to shave, shave. Take along some breath mints, but make sure they're not in your mouth during the interview. Have your hair neatly combed or brushed, and don't get extravagant. Smile during your interview. Speak clearly. Don't be afraid to take a few moments to gather yourself before answering a question.

Strategy #4: Be Sure About Your Answer

Don't say things like "Maybe" and "I might feel" because they sound wishy-washy. You want to be confident about how you feel about the questions because it shows an ability to think deeply and critically. Scholarships that require interviews generally are scholarships that will go to people who have the ability for independent thought. So if you go in and quote your parents for every answer, you're not going to do well. If you have conflicting thoughts about an issue, that's fine, but be confident in why you have conflicting thoughts and say so.

Strategy #5: Show the Interviewer Why You're a Good Investment

In a way, scholarships are like investments. At least, that's what it feels like for the people and institutions who give them out. They want scholarship money to go to people who are going to succeed. And although success can mean different things to different people, if you let the interviewer know you have goals, a plan to achieve them, and the will and desire to do so, you'll go a long way to getting a good score for your interview.

Strategy #6: Practice Under the Lights

We set up a little studio, which was actually just the corner of a room. We put in bright directional lamps and a video recorder on a tripod. Then we had our children practice giving answers while in a formal interview setting. The video recorder allows us to go back and see any gestures and tics that can detract from an interview (e.g., chewing fingernails, fussing with hair). Also, this gave our children the opportunity to start thinking about some of the more common interview questions.

Cash Clue

Practice answering standard interview questions. Write them down in essay form a few times to get the answers planted in your head.

The Importance of Video Sessions

We're going to talk a bit more about our sixth strategy. We believe it's very important to have a friend or family member ask you the sample questions in this chapter while making a video recording of your answers. Turn on all the lights in the room or use a spotlight in order to simulate the pressure of a real interview. Watch the video and look for ways to improve your performance. Anything you can change to make you appear more confident is a good thing. Repeat this process every few days, and you'll soon have the feeling that an interview is routine, and you won't feel the pressure that you otherwise might experience.

Scholarship Spotlight

If you're interested in fungus, there's a scholarship for you! The Mycological Society of America offers scholarships for researchers, teachers, and students who are involved in the study of mycology, or fungi (The Mycological Society of America, 2009). For more details, visit http://msafungi.org/msa-awards.

12

Tricks of the Trade

Whatever Works

WE'VE talked to a lot of students over the years, and we've found that what works for some doesn't necessarily work for others. Although we argue, for example, that the best approach is to hunt for as many appropriate scholarships as possible, we know of some students who spent their time finding the best potential match and going all out on those select few applications, and they were successful.

So, try our methods. Try out others' tricks. Find out what works for you.

Scholarship Spotlight

The Schering-Plough Will to Win program offers scholarships to high school seniors with asthma. Applicants should be determined, disciplined, and successful with managing their asthma. There are 10 scholarships of $5,000 each (Schering-Plough, 2009). For more details, visit http://www.schering-ploughwilltowin.com.

Overcoming Roadblocks

An interview is one thing you might have to get through in order to win a scholarship. There is, however, another thing we know you'll face on the road to college funding, and it's called a roadblock.

The process of applying for scholarships and college admission can be long and arduous. This can lead to frustration, which in turn can lead to missed opportunities, because it's easier to stop applying for scholarships after you've applied for a few. Moreover, if you've taken an extraordinary amount of time in filling out a particular form, say the FAFSA, then you'll find yourself having less time to fill out scholarship applications. For these reasons and more, it's good to have a strategy for overcoming roadblocks.

A roadblock is something that is stopping you from proceeding with whatever it is you're doing. It could be an application. It could be filling out a form. It could be obtaining information such as a parent's tax records. We hope you find our strategy useful in overcoming your own personal roadblocks on the path to scholarship funding.

Our strategy employs five steps:

1. *Recognize that you're at a roadblock*: This can be more difficult than it appears. You could tell yourself that you'll ask your parents later for copies of their tax records, and you'll jump ahead on the application to the

next section. It doesn't appear that you're at a stopping point. Although it's good to go ahead and fill out an application this way, it's important to write down what you've missed and to know what your roadblock is to completing the application.

2. *Identify the roadblock*: Skipping over a form or transcript that's needed is one thing. You can write down *need Dad's tax records*. But there are other roadblocks that are more subtle. For example, let's say you noticed a scholarship that applies to you, but you have to write an essay on a particular topic that you know nothing about, say native Hawaiian birds. You could shrug and move on to the next scholarship. Instead, write down *investigate Hawaiian birds* as a roadblock.

3. *Complete a to-do list*: Now that you have a roadblock identified, you will know what you need to overcome the roadblock. If you don't, solicit help from friends, faculty, and family until you do. Then put this item on a to-do list. You might, for example, write down *find last year's tax returns* or *locate last year's adjusted gross income* (AGI).

4. *Do the items on your to-do list*: There are people who take great delight in procrastinating, but procrastination won't win you any scholarship money. Make sure your to-do list is in a place you see every day, such as a refrigerator door. Then make sure the items get checked off as you complete them, and make sure the items on your list are completed at the earliest possible time, the following day if possible.

5. *Keep going once the roadblock is removed*: See how easy this is? You've already identified the roadblock and removed it. Now it's time to get right back to where the roadblock was and continue. If the roadblock was stopping you from completing an application or filling out the FAFSA, then get right back to the application or FAFSA and continue the process. You might run into another

roadblock, after all, and if you wait, it might cause you to miss a deadline.

Let's take a longer look at each of the steps in our strategy. We're doing this because we believe it's a vital process to keep you going in your pursuit of scholarship money. We've seen time and time again students who give up on applying for scholarships because it's too difficult a process, and we believe their lack of enthusiasm results from missing our first step, recognizing the roadblock.

Step #1: Recognize That You're at a Roadblock

Sometimes when we're sick, we'll notice the symptoms long before we realize we're sick. For example, it's easy to know if you have a headache, if you're feeling some muscle pains, but it might not dawn on you until later that you're coming down with the flu. Sooner or later, though, you'll realize you're sick!

When searching for college funding sources such as scholarships and proceeding down the road of gathering resources, filing your FAFSA, practicing your essay writing, or completing online scholarship applications, be aware of your feelings. Are you getting overly tired? Do you feel like you're getting sick of scholarships? Or maybe you're just sitting there, scratching your head, and not knowing why.

This could all be the result of a session you conducted yesterday, when you didn't know how to answer a particular question on the FAFSA. That's why you need to know you've come up against a roadblock. It will drain your energy quickly and you won't even know why, like why your head hurts before recognizing it as a symptom of the flu.

Step #2: Identify the Roadblock

Writing down the name of your roadblock will take you a long way in removing it. If you're stuck on a particular question in an application, identifying the roadblock is relatively easy. But as we pointed out earlier, sometimes it's more subtle.

We've found that sticky notes work great for identifying roadblocks. If it's a particular question on an application, write down the application and question, not just the question number. For example, you could write:

ROADBLOCK

Hawaii Audubon Scholarship, Question 29
What is unique about Hawaiian bird species? (And why should I care?)

Index cards also work well.

Now, put your identified roadblock on your refrigerator. Use a kitchen magnet if your roadblock is on an index card (we suggest using a magnet for sticky notes, too, so they don't fall off and get lost).

Step #3: Complete a To-Do List

Use another sticky note or index card for your to-do list. Write down specific, concrete action items of what you need to do in order to overcome the roadblock you identified in the previous step. A lot of times, your list might have just one item.

For example, you might come across an essay topic that gives you trouble, leaving you scratching your head, such as: Pick the person that inspires you the most and explain why he or she inspires you. You might not have a clear idea of an answer, so you could put down on your to-do list:

Write down the names of 10 people who inspire me.

Or, for example, you don't know much about your tax returns because one of your parents handles all of the tax filings or hires someone to do them. In this case, give your list more details so that you know precisely what to do.

1) Ask mom who files taxes.
2) Call the tax preparer.
3) Ask the tax preparer to send me a copy
of return, preferably by e-mail.

Now you've identified the roadblock and have come up with a plan for overcoming it.

Cash Clue

You might feel lost because you don't have enough information about something, even to the point of not being able to identify what it is that you don't know. For these situations, identify the roadblock as best you can and then put "research the topic online" on your to-do list.

Step #4: Do the Items on Your To-Do List

If you've already completed the other steps in the roadblock strategy, you might find that this step is easier to accomplish than you might've otherwise thought possible. This has been the case for us. We've found that by identifying the problem and writing down a to-do list, we are actually inspired to go ahead and do the item(s) right away! Maybe we just don't like clutter on our refrigerator door and want to get those sticky notes and index cards off.

Cash Clue

By writing down the roadblocks as you reach them, you avoid accumulating a long list of action items. If your to-do list approaches 30 items or more because of procrastination, you could easily lose your momentum in the hunt for scholarship money. Also, add a date to your to-do list so you'll know how many days go by without resolution.

Sometimes your to-do list has research items. There have been numerous times when we've forgotten how much information can be found online. If you can form the right question with the right key words, the answer usually shows up right away on a search engine.

If you can't get to your to-do list right away, it will be there in sight, on the refrigerator door, and you'll see it several times a day. Get in the habit of getting those roadblock and to-do sticky notes off the fridge as quickly as possible. Get a glass jar and stuff your vanquished roadblock notes in there so you can have a good visual image of how much progress you've made.

Step #5: Keep Going Once the Roadblock Is Removed

Removing a roadblock can be an accomplishment in itself, but remember that it was only something blocking you from achieving your goal. So immediately go back to that application or that form and complete it.

Remember that this is a process, and you need to keep working at it in order to keep the process moving. The process will result in scholarship money, so it's definitely a worthwhile pursuit!

Odds and Ends Tips

Over the years, we've uncovered a few tips and strategies that have helped us and our children find and win scholarships.

Make sure you schedule time each week for working on scholarship applications. Of course, the more time you can schedule, the better. But we understand how busy a high school student can be, so we suggest that as a minimum, schedule two nights a week for scholarship applications and plan for at least 2 hours for each session. This is, of course, after you get those first few scholarships out the door, which might take longer than your later applications.

Do you find yourself forgetting about things, maybe even your scheduled scholarship search sessions? We certainly find ourselves forgetting about things from time to time. That's why it's useful to set up reminders with your Internet browser or e-mail service. Computers often have applications that accomplish the same thing. Whichever reminder system you use, you'll be grateful you don't miss those deadlines when as a result!

Finally, if you get on a roll, and find yourself filling out applications with astute answers and are feeling confident, keep going! Just because you scheduled 2 hours for your application session, you don't have to stop after 2 hours are up. Keep going for another 30 minutes. You'll be ahead of the game for your next session.

Goal Setting

Goal setting is something we all do daily, whether it's preparing breakfast or getting through the workday. But it's important to understand what your goals are in relation to college scholarships.

The important aspect of our technique is that your goals need to be actionable and measurable. Let's give an example of an unspecific goal. Say, you tell yourself, "I want to work harder next week." Note that this is not a vague goal. It's just unspecific. What does "work harder" mean? Goals that are unspecific generally don't have much influence on our actions. And if they do, we have very little chance of gauging how well we achieved our goal.

But if you can be more specific, such as to tell yourself, "I want to cut my lunch hour short by 15 minutes so I can work on that report and get it out by the end of the week." Note that this is very specific, and it includes a way by which your goal is measured. If your report is out by the end of the week, your extra work will have succeeded. By having goals that are specific, we have a much better chance of influencing ourselves into achieving the goal.

Goal Setting and Scholarships

By setting a goal of two evenings (or more) per week of

scholarship searching and applications, you've set a specific goal. As you come across items on your to-do list, use the technique of goal setting to accomplish your items. As you progress in your search for scholarships, you might try to further refine your goals, such as completing two scholarship applications per scholarship session. As we've said before, whatever works for you is what you should be doing.

Miniature To-Do Lists

When you finish up your work for the night, whether it is essay writing, studying for the SAT, or filling out scholarship applications, you're usually at the top of your game. That is, you're scheduling (in your mind) what you need to do next. One of our favorite tricks (one we still employ), is to write a miniature to-do list. This helps us when we pick up working for the next day. We can hit the ground running, instead of taking those 10 to 15 minutes of finding our place again.

Scholarship Spotlight

The LaFontaine Aquatic Entomology Scholarship is offered from the Federation of Fly Fishers (FFF). This $500 scholarship is aimed at graduate students who are involved in the study of aquatic entomology, or insects that live in or near fresh water (Federation of Fly Fishers, 2009). For more details, visit http://www.fedflyfishers.org.

13

After the Money Rolls In

That First Scholarship

A **CONGRATULATIONS** letter with the announcement that you've won a scholarship award is a tremendous accomplishment. Go ahead and give a high five to your friends and family. Take the night off. Finished? OK, now back to work.

Seriously, we want to stress that it's great to pat yourself on the back with your successes. But we're equally serious that the job isn't finished. Until you've exhausted all of your potential scholarship sources, there are more to apply for.

And then there's next year, right?

Scholarship Spotlight

The Veterans of Foreign Wars of the United States (VFW) offers a number of scholarship programs, including the Voice of Democracy Scholarship Competition and an essay contest. These scholarship programs award more than $3.4 million in scholarships and incentives (Veterans of Foreign Wars of the United States, 2009). For more details, visit http://www.vfw.org.

The M in GRAND SLAM

*M*aintain your advantage by following up. There could be some scholarships that need you to send additional information. Do it immediately. Track the dates when funds are disbursed. And keep applying for scholarships. When you are awarded one scholarship, don't stop there. Keep going and maintain your advantage.

Scholarship Considerations

Read your scholarship award carefully. A scholarship is a type of contract, and now that you're an adult you are liable to abide by the terms. Here are some common requirements for keeping your scholarship in good standing (like we said, read yours several times to make sure you know how to stay within the guidelines).

Sometimes a scholarship will require you to send them a "Progress Report" periodically to remain eligible. This could be each semester, once a year, or a different time period; mark it on your calendar so you don't forget. Most scholarships require that you maintain a certain grade point average. Check it out and write it down in (you guessed it) a file or folder. Sometimes an award is given only for certain expenditures. If yours says it's for tuition only, don't spend any extra on housing or that new laptop you've been eyeing.

Check whether the award is tied to a certain major or school.

Sometimes once you get into college you decide that interior decorating isn't really your cup of tea and you want to switch to journalism as a major. Did you get a scholarship from "Beautiful Home Interiors of Mississippi" that is only eligible for interior decorating majors? If so, you might want to wait a year (or however long the award states it covers) before switching, or you'll probably have to return the money. Likewise, if the scholarship is tied to a specific school you'd better think twice before transferring.

Athletics is a whole different ball park. If you win an athletic award, you almost always have to play actively in the sport that the scholarship covers. Our son Scott had the option of accepting a basketball scholarship but ultimately decided he didn't want to invest the time that playing would take from his academic studies. As luck would have it, in October of his freshman year he dislocated his shoulder. If he'd have been attending on a basketball scholarship he would have been unable to play and could have lost his funding.

Check and see if the scholarship is renewable. Sometimes you will be eligible for the same scholarship each year for 4 years but you have to reapply each year. This happened to Scott when he won a U.S. Marine Corps award; he almost missed renewing it when he forgot to mark the deadline on his new calendar. Luckily his brother Alan applied for the same scholarship during his freshman year and was kind enough to remind him. Mind you, the award was "only" $2,700; multiply that by 4 years of school, however, and it's a tidy $10,800! Not too shabby for filling out a form once a year, don't you think?

Consider Next Year

Many scholarships are renewable, but you have to go through the application process again. Many of these will have a separate application for previous winners. As long as your basic information is the same and you've earned decent grades during your first year of college, you shouldn't have any problems winning the scholarship for each year you attend college.

But think about how much time you'll save if you have a manila folder or a computer folder that contains all of the information you used when applying for that particular scholarship. This is when you'll appreciate knowing which essay you used for this particular application so that you can write another essay along the same theme.

Remember to take your scholarship folders and files with you to school. You'll have time at college to continue to apply for scholarships. Because there are so many different sources of scholarships, the scholarship deadlines can be at different times of the year, although many fall in early spring.

We've seen firsthand from our children how beneficial it is to save all of the application information and keep it organized, because in ensuing years, applying for scholarships is a relative breeze.

Institutional Scholarships After Freshman Year

We encourage you to work hard during your freshman year at college. As our son Scott pointed out, if a student does really well in his freshman courses, sometime an institutional or departmental scholarship will open up. If you're a freshman at college and are getting outstanding grades, it can sometimes be financially rewarding to talk to the head of the department and ask about scholarship opportunities. In other circumstances, work-study programs are available. These not only help you to earn money, but work experience is a definite plus on scholarship applications and on resumes for college graduates. Many companies want workers who have experience, and many times, a student fresh out of college has none. A work-study program helps to correct this.

Keep Track of Money

You will want to keep track of college costs and where your college funding is coming from. Again, a journal works well for this. You might want to consider getting an accordion folder with at least four divisions, one for each year of college. You can put print-outs in your accordion folder; this way, you'll always know where you can go to make an accounting of your college costs and how those costs were paid for.

This also will be beneficial when you fill out scholarship applications next year. Some applications might ask about previous scholarships.

Besides, it's always a good idea to be able to look at a chart or graph and see where the money goes. People who work for a living are amazed at how quickly the money goes out the door, and many an adult wonders where it went.

Consider Postgraduate Work

You might be considering going on for a master's or doctoral degree. If so, it's even more important for you to keep track of your scholarships and college costs. You'll also want to keep all of your records from your undergraduate years. You'll be able to apply for scholarships for postsecondary degrees, but you'll have to supply additional information from your early college years.

The GRAND SLAM

We believe that our GRAND SLAM method will help you to win scholarship funding for your college education, and we'd like to reinforce what we've relayed to you in this book by repeating what each letter of GRAND SLAM stands for.

Get started now.
Research yourself, your interests, and your skills.
Analyze the fit/match between you and the college.
Navigate your way to scholarship money.
Develop an action plan.

*S*cholarships—find the ones you can win.
*L*earn how to write good essays.
*A*pply for scholarships and for admission to the college
that's right for you.
*M*aintain your advantage by following up.

Again, it's important to get started right away in the scholarship application process, or you'll kick yourself for missing deadlines. If you wait until there's the added pressure of an approaching deadline, your essays will likely not get the revisions they need and your answers will come across as hurried.

Research yourself, your interests, and your skills. As we've pointed out, many scholarship judges will award scholarships to those students who have a sense of self-confidence and self-awareness. Judges will be less likely to award money to students who are waffling on a career path or seem unsure about wanting to make a difference in the world. Don't underestimate the value that writing in your journals and examining yourself, your motives and feelings, can bring to the scholarship application process.

Analyze the fit/match between you and the college. By choosing a college that best fits your education and career needs, you'll find yourself more apt to win institutional scholarships. In addition, your college experience will more likely be a pleasant and rewarding one.

Navigate your way to scholarship money. That's right, scholarship money often is just a mouse-click away. We've given you websites that contain hundreds of scholarships you can apply for. We encourage you to narrow down your selections to the scholarships that apply most to you, but by using the Internet, you can travel far down the road to full college funding.

Develop an action plan. All of the theories and strategies in the world won't win you a dime of scholarship money. The trick is that you actually have to *do* things, you have to *act*. And this is where the action plan comes in. We can summarize it easily: Get started now and then keep going. The details of the plan simply make your actions more efficient (which of course we fully support).

Scholarships—apply for them and win them. It does no good to find scholarship sources and then not apply. And equally important, unless you finish the application and submit it, you're not going to win any scholarships. The trick here is to put together a *winning* application and then submit it.

Learn how to write good essays. Consider the scholarship judges who are looking at application after application. Most of these applications probably reveal a student who had decent grades and who wants to go to college and do well there. OK, so what is going to set your application apart from the others? The answer is your essay. Essays, we believe, are one of the most important factors that scholarship judges look at when deciding where the scholarship money will go.

Apply to the college that's right for you. If you want to attend a college that has very high entrance standards, don't feel discouraged. By putting together a winning admissions application, you can gain entrance. If you find that you're not interested in a wide-ranging 4-year education, that you want to simply learn a trade that you love and practice, then go for it! There are some students who claim that there's a stigma associated with not wanting to attend a 4-year degree college. Poppycock! If there's one thing that we as parents have learned, it's that every person is different, and every person's course to success lies down a separate path.

Maintain your advantage by following up. Once you start applying for scholarships, make sure you remain aware of dates when winners are announced. Also, if any scholarship application results in a request for additional information from you, it's vital that you make this your top priority. If you need to follow up with someone else for additional information so you can complete an application, make this a top priority, too. Following up can mean the difference between almost winning a scholarship and winning it outright.

Which brings us back to hitting that grand slam. By reading through the instructions for each letter of GRAND SLAM, you'll probably remember some of the tips and techniques presented in this book that applied to your particular situation. Remember that a grand slam is a base-clearing home run. You might win a scholarship or two, but then stop applying, figuring you've done your part. But you might not have your college costs fully covered yet. That's why you should go for the grand slam. Go for full funding for your college education. To do that, you have to keep searching for and winning scholarship money. We know you can do it!

A Few Parting Words

As parents, we were, of course, pleased in a financial sense that we were able to help our children fully fund their higher education with no financial help from us. And we've helped others along the way, too. But we'd like to point out an additional benefit that winning scholarships gives to high school students. It increases their sense of independence. We're strong believers in helping high school graduates go out into the real world and become adults, meaning that they don't have to rely on their parents for financial support. The sooner that high school graduates can be responsible for their own expenses, the sooner they'll become responsible adults. As parents, that seems to us to be a worthy goal.

We hope that your endeavors to find scholarship funds meet with great success, and we believe that if you follow the strategies we describe in this book, you'll hit your own scholarship GRAND SLAM!

Resources

College Planning Resources

Virtual College Tours

CampusTours

http://www.campustours.com

CampusTours provides virtual college tours and showcases other multimedia presentations from colleges and universities. They've been online since 1997.

eCampusTours.com

http://www.ecampustours.com

This is another virtual college tour website. This site also has information on college funding and contact information for colleges. They offer virtual tours of more than 1,200 college campuses.

CollegeWeekLive

http://www.collegeweeklive.com

This website showcases the latest innovation in college recruiting, offering information on virtual college fairs, during which students go online to chat live with admissions personnel and listen to expert advice.

College Admissions Tests

College Board

http://www.collegeboard.com

This is the website that is the springboard for students who are planning to take the SAT. It also is loaded with other helpful information on taking the test and attending college.

ACT, Inc.

http://www.act.org/aap

This is the home site for the organization that brings you the ACT test. It is the first stop for information on taking the ACT. It also has information for college administrators and students with disabilities.

Test Preparation and Essays

majortests.com

http://www.majortests.com

This site has helpful information on preparing for a number of entrance examinations. For students looking to prepare for essay writing, this site offers helpful information.

FreeSAT1Prep.com SAT Essay

http://www.sattest.us/writing

This site offers an outstanding overview of an approach to writing an SAT essay. For anyone preparing to take the SAT, this site provides valuable insights on what to expect.

College Board SAT Sample Essay

http://www.collegeboard.com/student/testing/sat/prep_one/essay/essay_6.html

This is a page on the College Board site that lists an essay that scored a perfect 6. It also offers an explanation for why the essay received the high score.

College Board Scoring Guide

http://www.collegeboard.com/student/testing/sat/about/sat/essay_scoring.html

This is a web page on the College Board site that students should visit because it offers a precise explanation on how the SAT essays are scored.

SparkNotes: Two Sample SAT Essays—Up Close

http://www.sparknotes.com/testprep/books/newsat/chapter6section5.rhtml

This is an excellent website for learning about how SAT essays are scored, and it lists the different grading criteria. This site will help students know how to prepare for writing high-scoring essays.

Funding and Financial Aid Resources

Financial Aid

Free Application for Federal Student Aid (FAFSA)

http://www.fafsa.ed.gov

This is the first stop for most students in their quest for financial aid. Many financial aid offices require the FAFSA to determine financial aid eligibility. There also is information on how to fill out the form. This form can be filled out online and saved for later completion.

Student Aid on the Web

http://studentaid.ed.gov

For federal student aid programs administered by the U.S. Department of Education, this is the site to visit. It includes information about the Academic Competitiveness Grants, the National Science and Mathematics

Access to Retain Talent Grant (National SMART), and Teacher Education Assistance for College and Higher Education Grant (TEACH Grant).

Federal Student Aid Gateway

http://federalstudentaid.ed.gov

As the name implies, this site is a gateway for federal financial aid. It provides information, guidance, and tools to help students find federal funding. It also has information for counselors and financial partners.

Information for Financial Aid Professionals

http://ifap.ed.gov/ifap/index.jsp

The Information for Financial Aid Professionals (IFAP) website consolidates information and resources for Title IV federal student aid. This site has information for the entire financial aid community.

Federal Pell Grant Program

http://www.ed.gov/programs/fpg

This is the website for the Federal Pell Grant Program, which provides need-based grants to promote access to postsecondary education.

U.S. Department of Education Office of Federal Student Aid

http://www.ed.gov/about/offices/list/fsa

This website is a great jumping-off point to learn about the different kinds of federal aid that are available.

Robert C. Byrd Honors Scholarship Program

http://www.ed.gov/programs/iduesbyrd/index.html

This website helps students apply for scholarships that are federally funded but are administered by states. The program is designed to recognize exceptional high school seniors who show promise in postsecondary education.

Federal Work-Study Program

http://www.ed.gov/programs/fws

This is the website of a program that provides funds to students through part-time employment. There are about 3,400 participating postsecondary institutions.

Federal Supplemental Educational Opportunity Grant (FSEOG)

http://www.ed.gov/programs/fseog

This site is the home of the FSEOG Program, which provides need-based grants to low-income undergraduate students.

Discretionary Grant Applications

http://www.ed.gov/fund/grant/apply/grantapps/index.html

This site provides a listing of grants that are provided via discretionary funds from the federal government.

Scholarships for Disadvantaged Students

http://bhpr.hrsa.gov/DSA/sds.htm

The Scholarships for Disadvantaged Students program provides scholarships to students from disadvantaged backgrounds. The students should be enrolled in health professions or nursing programs.

Student Gateway to the U.S. Government

http://www.students.gov

In addition to a section on paying for college, this site includes sections on planning for careers and has excellent overviews on government programs.

Financial Aid Resource Publications From the U.S. Department of Education

http://studentaid.ed.gov/students/publications/student_guide/index.html

The Department of Education publications site is helpful for students who are preparing for postsecondary education. The publications are focused on financial aid resources.

Loans

About Direct Loans

http://www.direct.ed.gov/about.html

This federal website has links and information about other sources of federal aid in addition to direct loans.

Federal Perkins Loan Program

http://www.ed.gov/programs/fpl

Perkins Loans are federal loans for college. The Federal Perkins Loan Program provides low-interest loans to help students finance the costs of postsecondary education.

Parent PLUS Loans

http://www.parentplusloan.com

Parent PLUS Loans are federal loans that help parents and guardians borrow funds to help their children attend undergraduate programs.

Federal Stafford Loans

http://www.staffordloan.com

This is the website for federal Stafford Loans. These loans are fixed-rate federal student loans for undergraduate and graduate students.

Federal Family Education Loan (FFEL) Program

http://www.ed.gov/programs/ffel

For federal loan program information, this is the website to visit. The FFEL includes four components: Stafford Loans, Unsubsidized Stafford Loans, Federal PLUS Loans, and Federal Consolidation Loans.

Direct Consolidation Loans

http://www.loanconsolidation.ed.gov

This is the home website for a program that pays off several types of federal education loans and creates one new loan that may have a lower rate than one or more of the underlying loans.

The Office of the Ombudsman

http://www.ombudsman.ed.gov

The Federal Student Aid Ombudsman of the Department of Education helps with disputes and other problems that concern federal student loans.

Scholarship Search Engines

NextStudent.com (States)

http://www.nextstudent.com/directory-of-scholarships/State/State-scholarships.aspx

> This is a scholarship search website provided by NextStudent.com that is categorized by states.

NextStudent.com (General Directory)

http://www.nextstudent.com/directory-of-scholarships

> This is a scholarship search website provided by NextStudent.com that is categorized by subjects other than states.

Online Education Database

http://oedb.org/scholarship

> At the Online Education Database website, you can search for scholarships by categories such as religious affiliation of the college.

FastWeb

http://www.fastweb.com

> This is a comprehensive scholarship search site online. Not only can you search for scholarships, but if you fill out your profile, FastWeb will send you e-mail alerts about new scholarships and deadlines.

FinAid!

http://www.finaid.org

> This is more than just a scholarship search engine. There also are cost estimators, information about loans and college savings, and tutorials to help you fill out forms. There also is information about locating college loans.

College Board Scholarship Search

http://apps.collegeboard.com/cbsearch_ss/welcome.jsp

> This search engine allows searching by location, cost, size, type of college, and more. Information on college-bound tests, planning for college, finding and applying to the right school as well as financial planning is provided.

CollegeNet

http://www.collegenet.com/elect/app/app

You can search for scholarships by either keyword or profile. There also are forums on the site, which sometimes contain useful threads.

SuperCollege.com

http://www.supercollege.com

SuperCollege has a scholarship search engine as well as a college search engine. There also is a large list of articles that can help you with your quest to fund your college education.

Careers and Colleges

http://www.careersandcolleges.com

As the name of this website implies, they focus on careers and colleges. You can use a tool on the website to assess your career plans. Of course, it wouldn't be complete without a scholarship search engine. This website claims to have more than 4,000 college profiles.

Scholarships.com

http://www.scholarships.com

Here is a website that delivers on its name, scholarships. The site claims to have information on more than $19 billion of scholarships in their listings. You can search for local, state, and federal scholarships that are based on your academic achievements as well as your talents. They also have a tool to create scholarship application request letters.

Yahoo Directory: Scholarship Programs

http://dir.yahoo.com/Education/Financial_Aid/Scholarship_Programs

This website doesn't have the same depth as other search engine website, but the scholarship opportunities on its list are excellent.

College Answer

http://www.collegeanswer.com/index.jsp

College Answer has an excellent search engine for scholarships. This site, an offshoot of Sallie Mae, also is loaded with information for the college-bound student.

The Multicultural Advantage Scholarships and Fellowships Search

http://www.multiculturaladvantage.com/scholarship.asp

Resource for grants, fellowships, and scholarships for college students of diverse backgrounds and on all academic levels.

Checklists

Grade Level Checklist

http://www.mtbaker.wednet.edu/career/grade.htm

This website offers checklists for high school students on how best to prepare for college, including suggested coursework and extracurricular activities. Lists are divided by grades 9–12. For high school students and guidance counselors planning ahead, these lists provide excellent resources.

EasyAid.com Financial Aid Checklist

http://www.easyaid.com/financial_aid_checklist.html

This is a straightforward checklist on applying for financial aid. The website also provides resources and links for all aspects of college admissions and funding.

Mrs. Erdvig's College Advisement Page

http://turnertechcap.com

This website is sponsored by the William H. Turner Technical Arts High School in Miami, FL. It has checklists for high school students, starting in the ninth grade. For anyone wanting to know what needs to be done to prepare for college, this is a great site to explore.

AIEmail

http://www.aie.org/AIEmail/Issues/20070827/index.cfm

This website provides a checklist for high school students by grade on steps to take in college planning. Visitors can sign up for a weekly e-mail newsletter. Resource links also are available.

Virginia Association of Financial Aid Administrators

http://www.vasfaa.org/docs/resources/justforparents.html

This website is designed for parents, but it also is a great resource for counselors. It has a calendar of events that students and parents should be doing to prepare high school children for college. The lists are organized by grades 9–12.

Higher Education Services Corporation High School Calendar

http://www.hesc.com/content.nsf/SFC/1/High_School_Calendar

This is a site geared toward New York students, but the calendar for high school juniors and seniors is excellent. It is helpful for parents, counselors, and students alike.

FinAid! Student's Financial Aid Checklist

http://www.finaid.org/students/checklist.phtml

FinAid! provides a calendar checklist of the steps in applying for financial aid.

Financial Aid Evaluations

College Answer: Evaluating Award Letters

http://www.collegeanswer.com/deciding/award_comparison/ac_select.jsp

This website offers an online financial aid analyzer to evaluate financial aid award packages.

FinAid!: Guide to Financial Aid Award Letters

http://www.finaid.org/fafsa/awardletters.phtml

FinAid! provides a detailed look at financial award letters and packages. It also offers web resources for students and educators alike.

Financial Aid Facts

http://www.finaidfacts.org/how_much.htm

This site provides an analysis of college costs and financial aid and shows how to do the math in calculating the Unmet Financial Need (UFN).

OefftoCollege.com

http://www.offtocollege.com

OfftoCollege.com has numerous worksheets for college admissions and financial aid calculations. This site includes search engines for colleges and scholarships. The worksheets can be downloaded and printed.

College Board: EFC Calculator Help

http://www.collegeboard.com/student/pay/calc/efc_help.html

This is a detailed look at how to calculate the Expected Family Contribution (EFC), which is used to determine financial aid needs. It also is valuable in preparing to file the FAFSA.

College Foundation of North Carolina (CFNC)

http://www.cfnc.org/paying/packages.jsp

CFNC provides sample financial aid packages from fictitious colleges and compares the costs to the student.

Athletic Scholarships

The College Recruiting Group

http://www.playcollegesports.com

The College Recruiting Group helps high school athletes to be proactive in prompting colleges and universities to recruit them for athletic scholarships.

Varsityedge.com

http://www.varsityedge.com

This website offers information about the recruiting process for collegiate sports. It includes resources for how to make a recruiting video.

Tips for Making a Great Sports Recruiting Video

http://www.ex-designz.net/articleread.asp?aid=1626

This article offers helpful tips for how to make a sports recruiting video and what mistakes to avoid.

College Funding, State by State

Alabama

Alabama Mentor.org

http://www.alabamamentor.com/FinAid

This site provides information and applications for admission to Alabama universities and colleges.

Alabama Commission on Higher Education

http://www.ache.state.al.us/StudentAsst

This site offers information on the Alabama Student Grant and Assistance Programs, National Guard Educational Assistance Program, Police Officers' and Firefighters' Survivors' Educational Assistance Program, and a technology scholarship for teachers.

Alaska

AlaskAdvantage Education Grant

http://alaskadvantage.state.ak.us/page/276

Details on a specific Alaska grant and scholarship programs are included on this site.

University of Alaska (UA) Scholars Program

http://www.alaska.edu/scholars

This program encourages Alaska's middle and high school students to achieve higher academic excellence.

Arizona

Arizona Commission for Postsecondary Education

http://www.azhighered.gov

The goal of this commission is to help students and families plan for, enter, and succeed in higher education by accessing the optimum amount of grant and scholarship monies available.

High Honors Tuition Scholarship

http://www.ade.state.az.us/asd/tuitionwaiver

This scholarship offers qualified honors students a full state university tuition waiver valid for one year following graduation from high school.

Professional Student Exchange Program (PSEP)

http://wiche.edu/sep/psep

This program, sponsored by the Western Interstate Commission for Higher Education, offers out-of-state college or university degree programs at a reduced tuition rate for eligible Arizona residents.

Arkansas

Fund My Future

http://www.fundmyfuture.info

This site includes a scholarship search engine as well as a "backpack account" that saves results from your scholarship searches.

Arkansas Department of Higher Education

http://www.adhe.edu

This site provides information on higher education services for Arkansas residents and includes an extensive financial aid section.

California

California Student Aid Commission

http://www.csac.ca.gov/doc.asp?id=33

This site provides links and information on a variety of programs that are administered by the Student Aid Commission.

CalGrants.org

http://www.calgrants.org

This site offers information on state grants to attend a California college, university, career, or technical school.

California State Scholarships

http://www.peocalifornia.org/ca-scholarships.html

The California State Chapter of P.E.O. provides educational scholarships to California women studying in a variety of fields.

Colorado

CollegeInColorado.org

http://www.collegeincolorado.org/home.aspx

The site includes articles and information on planning for, applying to, and paying for college on Colorado. It also includes campus tours and online college applications.

Colorado Department of Higher Education

http://www.state.co.us/cche

Users can find information for state college resources for all public and private schools in Colorado. Information also is offered in Spanish on this site.

Colorado Educational Services & Development Association

http://www.cesda.org

CESDA provides education and support for the community on the college process to help Colorado residents apply for and attend college.

Connecticut

Connecticut Department of Higher Education

http://www.ctdhe.org

This site has a variety of links regarding topics like financial aid and Connecticut colleges. It also has information for alternate certificate routes and occupational schools.

Connecticut Talent Assistance Cooperative

http://www.conntacinc.org

This cooperative facilitates the entry or reentry into postsecondary education programs for all Connecticut residents.

CTMentor.org

http://www.ctmentor.org

This site is an online resource for applications and information for Connecticut universities and colleges.

Delaware

Delaware Higher Education Commission

http://www.doe.k12.de.us/infosuites/students_family/dhec

This commission administers 23 state-sponsored financial aid programs and 8 private scholarship programs.

SEED Scholarship

http://seedscholarship.delaware.gov

Student Excellence Equals Degree (SEED) provides tuition for full-time students enrolled in an associate's degree program at Delaware Technical & Community College or the Associate of Arts program at the University of Delaware.

District of Columbia

Office of the State Superintendent of Education

http://www.seo.dc.gov/seo

This office administers all of the District of Columbia's higher education grant programs.

Florida

Office of Student Financial Assistance

http://www.floridastudentfinancialaid.org

This office, part of the Florida Department of Education, facilitates the Federal Family Education Loan Program as well as Florida's grant and scholarship programs.

Georgia

Georgia Student Finance Commission

http://www.gsfc.org

This site provides information on state scholarships, grants, loans, and cancelable loans.

GACollege411

http://www.gacollege411.org

This site offers advice for planning for college in Georgia and information for students in middle and high school as well as for parents and educators.

Hawaii

GEAR UP Hawai'i

http://gearup.hawaii.edu

GEAR UP's mission is to encourage Hawaii's students to pursue college and career choices. The site offers guidance on how to apply to and pay for college.

University of Hawai'i System Financial Aid

http://www.hawaii.edu/admissions/aid.html

This site provides both need-based and merit-based financial aid information as well as aid based on geography, chosen major, and other criteria.

Hawai'i Community Foundation

http://www.hawaiicommunityfoundation.org

The foundation is the second largest provider of postsecondary scholarships in the state.

Idaho

Idaho State Board of Education

http://www.boardofed.idaho.gov/scholarships

The Idaho State Board of Education site provides links to scholarships, grants, loans, and other programs available to Idaho residents.

Illinois

Illinois Student Assistance Commission College Zone

http://www.collegezone.com

> College and career information for Illinois students can be found at this site, along with financial aid calculators, scholarship searches, and information on legislation that affects students.

Indiana

The State Student Assistance Commission of Indiana

http://www.in.gov/ssaci

> This commission makes college more affordable by providing need-based and achievement-based funds for those attending public, proprietary, and independent colleges.

Iowa

Robert D. Blue Scholarship

http://www.rdblue.org

> This scholarship fund was established to encourage the youth in Iowa to attend college in their home state.

Iowa College Student Aid Commission

http://www.iowacollegeaid.gov

> Aids in choosing a career and a major as well as Iowa college funding sources are offered at this site, along with "real advice" from current students.

Kansas

Kansas Board of Regents

http://www.kansasregents.org

> This site offers a guide to student loans, grants, scholarships, and awards as well as college planning for Kansas students.

Kentucky

Kentucky Council on Postsecondary Education
http://cpe.ky.gov/forstudents

The council helps Kentuckians follow the correct steps to attending college. Its website includes information for middle and high school students and also for transfer students on planning for college, paying for college, choosing majors, and adult education.

GoHigher Kentucky
http://www.gohigherky.org

This organization offers advice on college, careers, adult education, and planning for and selecting educational options. You can build a profile and save it for later use.

Kentucky Higher Education Assistance Authority
http://www.kheaa.com

This site provides guidance on planning and paying for college in Kentucky, with specific links for adult education and planning transfers and commonly asked questions by students.

Louisiana

Louisiana Office of Student Financial Assistance
http://www.osfa.state.la.us

This site details college savings plans, scholarships, grants, and loans available to Louisiana residents.

Maine

Finance Authority of Maine (FAME)
http://www.famemaine.com/education

FAME is committed to helping students plan for college in Maine, with calculators, an online scholarship search engine, and other tools for Maine residents.

Maryland

Maryland Higher Education Commission

http://www.mhec.state.md.us/financialAid

This site gives information on grants, scholarships, awards, and loans to help pay for higher education. The commission also offers presentations on "Money for College" throughout the year to Maryland students.

Massachusetts

Massachusetts Office of Student Financial Assistance

http://www.osfa.mass.edu

This office promotes access to higher education through early awareness programs and by making financial aid options available to Massachusetts residents.

Michigan

The Michigan Higher Education Student Loan Authority (MHESLA)

http://www.michigan.gov/mistudentaid

This site discusses Michigan financial aid programs, including grants, scholarships, loans, and savings plans. It also offers interesting articles to students on topics like tax breaks for education.

Minnesota

Get Ready for College

http://www.getreadyforcollege.org

Information on college preparation, planning, selection, and financial aid in Minnesota is provided at this site, along with a handy calendar of important dates.

Minnesota Office of Higher Education

http://www.ohe.state.mn.us

This site provides program criteria and rules for state financial programs that provide loans, grants, and work opportunities for state residents.

Mississippi

Rise Up!

http://www.mississippi.edu/riseupms/financialaid-state.php

This is a one-stop website where students can fill out one application for all state aid programs in Mississippi.

Missouri

Missouri Department of Higher Education

http://www.dhe.mo.gov

Information on planning, preparing, and paying for college in the state of Missouri can be found at this site.

Missouri Department of Higher Education

http://highered.mo.gov/ProgramInventory/search.jsp

This site hosts a scholarship search engine for Missouri students.

Montana

Student Assistance Foundation of Montana

http://www.safmt.org

This site provides career information as well as college entrance and financial aid information.

Montana Guaranteed Student Loan Program (MGSLP)

http://www.mgslp.state.mt.us

This organization works to improve access to college in Montana by offering variety of state and federal grants and loans, as well as information on student loans.

Nebraska

Nebraska's Coordinating Commission for Postsecondary Education (CCPE)

http://www.ccpe.state.ne.us/publicdoc/ccpe/financialaid.asp

This page contains frequently asked questions about financial aid in Nebraska and links to funding and scholarship programs for Nebraska students.

Nevada

Nevada System of Higher Education

http://system.nevada.edu

This site includes information and resources for Nevada students, such as the Millennium Scholarship Program, Nevada Prepaid Tuition, and INVest.

Nevada Department of Education

http://nde.doe.nv.gov/Students.html

This site provides resources for students of all ages who are planning postsecondary education in Nevada.

New Hampshire

New Hampshire Higher Education Assistance Foundation

http://www.nhheaf.org

The foundation provides students with everything they need to plan for college, from admission requirements to scholarships and grants available.

New Hampshire Postsecondary Education Commission

http://www.nh.gov/postsecondary

This commission is a coordinating agency that works with colleges, universities, and career schools in all sectors to enable students to access the financial aid available.

New Jersey

New Jersey Higher Education Student Assistance Authority
http://www.hesaa.org

> This organization provides students with the information and financial resources necessary to pursue their higher education goals.

New Mexico

New Mexico Higher Education Department
http://fin.hed.state.nm.us

> This site is dedicated to helping New Mexico students find the necessary funds to attend college. It provides an overview of the different types of aid available in the state.

New York

New York Higher Education Services Corporation
http://www.hesc.com

> This organization offers loan management services and college guidance as well as administers a variety of state and federal scholarships and grants.

Tuition Assistance Program
http://www.tapweb.org/totw

> This page directs students to the online application for New York's Tuition Assistance Program (TAP).

North Carolina

North Carolina State Education Assistance Authority
http://www.ncseaa.edu

> This is a state agency that administers programs that are designed to help college students pay for their education costs.

College Foundation of North Carolina

http://www.cfnc.org

This comprehensive site allows students and parents to plan for college and apply for scholarships and grants.

North Dakota

North Dakota University System

http://www.ndus.edu

This state resource page can help students determine the cost of college as well as find information on state and federal grants and scholarships.

Ohio

Ohio Board of Regents

http://regents.ohio.gov/sgs/index.php

This site contains a variety of state grant and scholarship programs open to residents of Ohio as well as links to other sources of financial aid.

Oklahoma

Oklahoma State Regents for Higher Education

http://www.okhighered.org

This site provides a wealth of information on Oklahoma's public universities and colleges as well as information on preparing for college and student aid.

Oregon

GetCollegeFunds.org

http://www.getcollegefunds.org

Students can find student financial aid, grants, and scholarship opportunities administered by the Oregon Student Assistance Commission on this site.

Oregon Student Assistance Commission

http://www.osac.state.or.us

This site offers information on state scholarship programs as well as a series of useful tip sheets to help in preparing for college.

Pennsylvania

Pennsylvania Higher Education Assistance Agency (PHEAA)

http://www.pheaa.org

One of the largest full-service financial aid organizations in the country, this organization's site covers state grants and financial aid processing.

Rhode Island

College Planning Center of Rhode Island

http://www.cpcri.org

This center offers expert guidance on all aspects of attending college in Rhode Island, from initial planning to financial aid.

RIscholarships.com

http://www.rischolarships.com

This site is a free search engine of Rhode Island scholarships from both state and private sectors.

Rhode Island State Grant Program

http://www.riheaa.org/borrowers/grants

This program provides need-based grants as well as scholarships and federal loan programs to students in Rhode Island.

South Carolina

South Carolina Commission on Higher Education

http://www.che.sc.gov

This site includes information for South Carolina students on attending college and finding financial aid as well as applications for state scholarships and grants.

South Carolina Higher Education Tuition Grants Commission

http://www.sctuitiongrants.com

This commission provides need-based grant assistance to eligible under-graduates attending South Carolina nonprofit, in-state colleges.

South Dakota

South Dakota Department of Education

http://doe.sd.gov/parents

This site contains information on state colleges and universities as well as scholarships available to South Dakota residents.

Tennessee

Tennessee Student Assistance Corporation

http://www.state.tn.us/tsac

This is the state resource page for information on financing your college education in Tennessee.

Texas

College for All Texans Foundation

http://www.collegeforalltexans.com

This comprehensive site includes information for planning and paying for your college education in the state of Texas, along with other tools like a college match-up feature.

Texas Guaranteed Tuition Plan

http://www.tgtp.org/aid.html

This plan allows Texans to prepay for college tuition and fees at today's rate. The Financial Aid page provides information on scholarships, grants, and the Texas Guaranteed Tuition Plan for all Texas residents.

Utah

Utah Higher Education Assistance Authority
http://www.uheaa.org

This site includes information on college planning, budget worksheets, calculators, and brochures for Utah college students.

Utah Mentor
http://www.utahmentor.org

This site covers topics like choosing a career, planning and preparing for college, selecting a school, and finding financial aid in Utah.

Utah System of Higher Education
http://www.utahsbr.edu

This site includes links to all 10 colleges and universities in Utah, with financial aid pages on each site.

Vermont

Vermont Government Education Website
http://www.vermont.gov/portal/education

Information on colleges, universities, continuing education, and financial aid for residents of Vermont is provided at this site.

Vermont Student Assistance Corp.
http://services.vsac.org/wps/wcm/connect/vsac/VSAC

This is a comprehensive state site that covers grants, scholarships, loans, applications, career planning, and much more.

Virginia

State Council of Higher Education for Virginia (SCHEV)
http://www.schev.edu

This site includes information on colleges, grants, scholarships, loans, and other means of financial aid for students in Virginia.

VirginiaMentor

http://www.virginiamentor.org

Finding a career, planning for college, financial resources, and search engines for Virginia residents are just a few of the topics covered at this site.

Washington

Washington Higher Education Coordinating Board

http://www.hecb.wa.gov

This site gives financial aid information for students and parents in the state of Washington.

West Virginia

West Virginia Higher Education Policy Commission

http://wvhepcnew.wvnet.edu

This site offers a direct link to each of West Virginia's public colleges and universities, as well as information on financial aid.

Wisconsin

Wisconsin Higher Educational Aids Board

http://heab.state.wi.us

This board sponsors state programs of financial aid, including scholarships, grants, loans, and tuition reciprocity programs in Wisconsin.

Wyoming

Wyoming Community College Commission

http://www.communitycolleges.wy.edu

This site is a comprehensive guide to Wyoming's seven community colleges that outlines degrees available as well as industry-specific programs.

University of Wyoming Office of Student Financial Aid

http://uwadmnweb.uwyo.edu/sfa

This site details financial aid awards available through the University of Wyoming.

References

Alliance for Young Artists & Writers. (2009). *Scholarships*. Retrieved from http://www.artandwriting.org/resources.htm

Alzheimer's Foundation of America. (2009). *AFA teens for Alzheimer's awareness college scholarship*. Retrieved from http://afateens.org/about_new.html

American Fire Sprinkler Association. (2009). *Complete contest information*. Retrieved from http://www.afsascholarship.org/information.htm

American Planning Association. (2009). *Scholarships*. Retrieved from http://planning.org/scholarships/index.htm

American Sheep Association. (2009). *MIWW contest information*. Retrieved from http://www.sheepusa.org/MIWW_Contest_Information

American Society for Enology and Viticulture. (2009). *Scholarship program*. Retrieved from http://asev.org/scholarship-program

The Association of Firearm and Tool Mark Examiners. (2009). *AFTE scholarship program*. Retrieved from http://www.afte.org/AssociationInfo/a_scholarship.htm

Ayn Rand Foundation. (2009). *Essay contests*. Retrieved from http://www.aynrand.org/site/PageServer?pagename=education_contests_index

Berger, S. L. (2006). *College planning for gifted students.* Waco, TX: Prufrock Press.

Berger, S. L. (2008). *The ultimate guide to summer opportunities for teens.* Waco, TX: Prufrock Press.

Body by Milk. (2009). *Sammy scholarship.* Retrieved from http://www. bodybymilk.com/sammy_scholarship.php

Bureau of Labor Statistics. (2009). *College enrollment and work activity of 2008 high school graduates.* Retrieved from http://www.bls.gov/ news.release/hsgec.nr0.htm

Chany, K. A., & Martz, G. (2006). *Paying for college without going broke.* New York, NY: Princeton Review.

Clark, K. (2009, September). New college scholarships for laid-off workers. *U.S. News & World Report,* 42.

The Coca-Cola Scholars Foundation. (2009). *Overview.* Retrieved from https://www.coca-colascholars.org

Common Knowledge Scholarship Foundation. (2009). *Scholarships based on what you know.* Retrieved from http://www.cksf.org/ hschool.cfm#free

Day, J. C., & Newburger, E. C. (2002). *The big payoff: Educational attainment and synthetic estimates of work-life earnings* (Current Population Reports, Special Studies, P23-210). Washington, DC: Commerce Dept., Economics and Statistics Administration, Census Bureau.

Duck brand duct tape stuck at prom scholarship winners. (2009). Retrieved from http://www.stuckatprom.com/contests/prom

Federation of Fly Fishers. (2009). *Award criteria.* Retrieved from http:// www.fedflyfishers.org/Default.aspx?tabid=4366

The Glen Miller Birthplace Foundation. (2009). *Scholarships.* Retrieved from http://www.glennmiller.org/scholarships.html

Illinois Student Assistance Commission. (2009). *Average cost of college.* Retrieved from http://www.collegezone.com/416_890.htm

Kaplan, B. (2002). *How to go to college almost for free.* New York, NY: HarperCollins.

Klingon Language Institute. (2009). *KLI academic award: The Kor memorial scholarship.* Retrieved from http://www.kli.org/scholarship

Kodak. (2009). *Eastman scholarship program.* Retrieved from http://motion.kodak.com/US/en/motion/Education/ Discounts_And_Scholarships

McNeil Consumer Healthcare. (2009). *2009 Tylenol scholarship.*

Retrieved from http://www.tylenol.com/page.jhtml?id=tylenol/
news/subptyschol.inc#

Michigan Llama Association. (2009). *MLA mission statement.* Retrieved
from http://www.michiganllama.org/about.html

Muratori, M. C. (2007). *Early entrance to college.* Waco, TX: Prufrock
Press.

The Mycological Society of America. (2009). *MSA awards.* Retrieved
from http://msafungi.org/msa-awards

National Potato Council. (2009). *Scholarship program.* Retrieved
from http://www.nationalpotatocouncil.org/NPC/programs_
scholarshipprogram.cfm?cache=050909115514

Pope, L. (2007). *Looking beyond the Ivy League: Finding the college
that's right for you.* New York, NY: Penguin.

Rye, D. (2001). *The complete idiot's guide to financial aid for college.*
New York, NY: Penguin.

Schering-Plough. (2009). *About the scholarship.* Retrieved from http://
www.schering-ploughwilltowin.com/about.asp

Siemens Corporation. (2009). *About the competition.* Retrieved from
http://www.siemens-foundation.org/en/competition.htm

Simpson, C. G., & Spencer, V. G. (2009). *College success for students
with learning disabilities.* Waco, TX: Prufrock Press.

Snyder, T. D., Dillow, S. A., & Hoffman, C. M. (2009). *Digest of Education
Statistics 2008* (NCES 2009-020). Washington, DC: National Center
for Education Statistics.

SVC Foundation. (2009). *Scholarship fund.* Retrieved from http://www.
svc.org/SF/SVCFoundationSchol.html

Truman Scholarship Foundation. (2009). *For candidates.* Retrieved
from http://www.truman.gov/candidates/candidates.htm

Veterans of Foreign Wars of the United States. (2009). *VFW scholarship
programs.* Retrieved from http://www.vfw.org/index.cfm?fa=cmty.
levelc&cid=1836&cfid=26501068&cftoken=14203786

Wei, C. C., Berkner, L., He, S., Lew, S., Cominole, M., & Siegel, P. (2009).
*2007–08 National Postsecondary Student Aid Study: Student financial
aid estimates for 2007–08: First look* (NCES 2009-166). Washington,
DC: National Center for Education Statistics.

Wissner-Gross, E. (2006). *What colleges don't tell you (and other
parents don't want you to know).* New York, NY: Hudson Street
Press.

About the Authors

DOUG and Robin Hewitt were both born and raised in Mt. Clemens, MI. They were friends throughout high school, but graduation set them on long, separate journeys. After 29 years, they found each other again. When they did, they married and became a husband-and-wife writing team living in Mayodan, NC (with a boxer mix named Rosie).

Doug is the author of the parenting book *The Practical Guide to Weekend Parenting: 101 Ways to Bond With Your Children While Having Fun*. Doug's parenting book was a result of his experiences as a divorced dad who did most of his parenting on the weekends. When Doug remarried, he "inherited" three grandchildren and realized that grandchildren look up to their grandparents in very special ways. These relationships provided the impetus for Doug and Robin's coauthored book, *The Joyous Gift of Grandparenting: 101 Practical Ideas & Meaningful Activities to Share Your Love*.

Doug and Robin took their experiences as parents and applied them to the special roles that high school guidance counselors and college financial administrators adopt when guiding students into higher education. Along the way, they learned to address the landmines that litter the road on the way to college and career.

With five children between them, Doug and Robin helped guide their offspring into higher education—at no cost to them. Their experience with research and with helping children face career considerations gave them crucial insights into finding college funding—and their children benefited. Thomas is a criminal justice major with an education fully funded by the GI Bill. Grace is majoring in photography and is funded by private scholarships. Lynn has a full teaching fellowship along with a number of other scholarships. Scott studies physics and has his college costs funded by the state because he graduated from a premier science and math boarding school. Alan is using his music skills to win scholarships while pursuing a music degree for teaching.

Doug has a master's degree in liberal studies. He also has attended extensive classroom courses in children psychology, sociology, and other fields of study relating to the raising of children. Both Doug and Robin understand the nuances of decisions that children must make with regard to careers and colleges. While Doug handles the creative aspect of authoring, Robin is a full-time freelance writer and coordinates the behind-the-scenes aspects of researching each writing project as well as shaping the manuscripts with her editing skills. They currently are working on a book about last-minute applications to college as well as the first two volumes in a series of *Microsoft Office for Beginners* books.